OLD AS THE HILLS

Also by Steven D. Price

TEACHING RIDING AT SUMMER CAMPS

PANORAMA OF AMERICAN HORSES

GET A HORSE!
Basics of Backyard Horsekeeping

TAKE ME HOME
The Rise of Country-and-Western Music

THE SECOND-TIME-SINGLE MAN'S
SURVIVAL GUIDE
(*with William J. Gordon*)

STEVEN D. PRICE

OLD AS THE HILLS

THE STORY OF BLUEGRASS MUSIC

The Viking Press | **New York**

First published in 1975 by The Viking Press, Inc.
625 Madison Avenue, New York, N.Y. 10022
Published simultaneously in Canada by
The Macmillan Company of Canada Limited

LIBRARY OF CONGRESS CATALOGING IN PUBLICATION DATA
Price, Steven D
  Old as the hills.

  Discography and bibliography: p.
  1. Bluegrass music—United States— History and
criticism. I. Title.
ML3561.B62P7   780'.42   74-20637
ISBN 0-670-52204-X

Second Printing April 1975
Printed in U.S.A.

PREFACE

As a string band might kick off a performance with a few words to the audience, let me say a few things at the outset about this book.

Old as the Hills is intended to be an introduction to string-band music. It is by no means an exhaustive study, nor does it come close to mentioning everyone who has been a part of professional Bluegrass. Such an undertaking would have resulted in a Burke's Peerage beyond the interest of all but the most serious students, who probably know already where to find such material. Musicians and bands found in these pages are either landmark figures or representatives of certain aspects of string-band music; often they are both. Anyone wanting to delve more deeply could do no better than to look into the magazines listed in Chapter Eight or to read the books mentioned in the Appendix. The definitive history of Bluegrass has yet to be written, and I hope that this book will encourage such a project.

The origins of Bluegrass are nearly four hundred years old and developed as a result of political, economic, and social events. Accordingly, a chronological approach to the book seemed most sensible. From back-porch amateurs to professional musicians, from barn raisings and medicine shows, to records, radio, and movies, from east Tennessee to West Germany, this brand of music has spanned the world as well as the centuries.

Not everyone agrees on what Bluegrass is. Purists feel that it must be played on unamplified instruments, that Bluegrass and electricity mix like oil and water. But there are many who don't, and to avoid an overly narrow definition problem, the book acknowledges (and appreciates) the existence of "rock-grass" performers.

That words are metaphors is no more evident than in writing about music. Using your ears as well as your eyes is essential, for how else can you find out about syncopations and slurs, hear what a "high lonesome" sounds like, or recognize the characteristics of trio and quartet harmonies? The Appendix at the back of the book includes a discography, but approach it with this word of caution: don't expect to locate every album (or even most of them) very easily. Bluegrass is not the kind of music that keeps most record shops in business. Your search might include inquiries at public and university libraries where record collections frequently include such "esoterica."

Finally, and on a personal note, working on this book has been, to use a pickers' expression, "a hoss and a half." I discovered Bluegrass at the college I attended, located considerably north of the Mason-Dixon Line. Therefore, to have met Bluegrass musicians in the course of this book's preparation touched off a certain nostalgia of joining a group, listening to records, learning the tunes, and performing them for our own amusement and at folk festivals. With these memories in the back of my mind, meeting my "folk heroes" and hearing them talk about their lives and craft added an unexpected dimension to the appreciation of string-band music and its practitioners with which I come away from this book.

ACKNOWLEDGMENTS

If everyone who participated in the preparation of this book were to take a bow, the show would last longer than a weekend festival. Among them are:

In Nashville, Bob Pinson and the staff of the Country Music Foundation, Bud Wendell of the Grand Ole Opry, and Jan and Jim Talley.

In England, Tony Russell of *Old Time Music.*

Musicians who were good enough to furnish me with information about themselves and their music: James Bailey, Curly Ray Cline, Bill Clifton, Johnny Dacus, Jerry Douglas, Bill Harrell, Vic Jordan, the Lewis Family, Jimmy Martin, Jim and Jesse McReynolds, Bobby Osborne, Don Reno, Buck Ryan, the Earl Scruggs Revue, Ricky Skaggs, Ralph Stanley, Roger Sprung, Charlie Waller, and Bill Yates.

Doug Tuchman, for his invaluable assistance.

Fred Bartenstein of *Muleskinner News,* for his many suggestions and corrections.

Steve Arkin, whose knowledge is reflective and reflexive.

David Robinson, a dynamite banjo picker and a patient teacher.

Jeanne and Merrill Pollack, mountaineers *manqués* at the start who have now headed for the hills.

Barbara Burn, for her editorial picking.

Susan Marx, who listened to innumerable hours of string-band music with a saintly patience and who read these pages with a super-critical eye.

CONTENTS

OLD AS THE HILLS

ONE **THEY CALL IT BLUEGRASS**

Bluegrass. To horsemen the word conjures up Kentucky's lush pastureland, the breeding ground of champion thoroughbreds. Botanists know it as the genus *Poa*. But to music lovers, particularly country-music fans, Bluegrass * is something else. It's twanging banjos, whining fiddles, sliding Dobro guitars, fluttering mandolins, and the solid rhythm of acoustic guitars and bass fiddles. It is also piercing solo singing and the tight harmonies of trio and quartet chorus harmonies. Bluegrass is romp-and-stomp instrumental tunes, mournful ballads of unrequited love and the homely virtues, and hymns of steadfast faith. It's part of a musical tradition spanning centuries, from the Elizabethan "Barbara Allen" to the Beatles' "Yesterday."

Once exclusively the bailiwick of America's rural South, Bluegrass has become a national, even international, institution. Millions have heard it on the sound tracks of *Bonnie and Clyde, Deliverance,* and *Payday,* as well as on television's *Beverly Hillbillies* and *Petticoat Junction.* Bluegrass is also featured amid the Dogpatch humor of *Hee Haw* and on other country-music radio and television programs. In a strictly commercial vein, radio and TV advertisements extol the qualities of automobiles, soft drinks, beer, and foodstuff against a background of banjos and fiddles.

Hearing the music live is no more difficult. Bands perform at roadside taverns and major concert halls, at

---

* Some people spell it "Blue Grass" or "bluegrass." I chose the capitalized one-word form, to distinguish the music from the name of its eponymous band, the Blue Grass Boys.

campus auditoriums and night clubs. Bluegrass festivals and conventions, more than 175 of them, take place all over the United States. Travelers in Europe and Asia will find touring American groups as well as local bands at concerts and festivals.

Although most people recognize the music when they hear it, what exactly *is* Bluegrass? Musicologists offer the following definition: Bluegrass is polyphonic vocal and instrumental music played on certain unamplified instruments, based on music brought from the British Isles to Appalachian regions and refined by additions of Negro and urban music. A Bluegrass band typically consists of a five-string banjo and guitar, together with a fiddle, Dobro guitar, mandolin, and bass fiddle (or any combination thereof). Vocal lead parts are rendered in the high-pitched style of traditional British balladry, with chorus harmonies added by a "high tenor" sung a third or fifth above the lead, and lower baritone and / or bass lines.

Although this definition would satisfy purists, there are exceptions that do more than prove the rule, they expand it. Some bands include drums, electric guitars, and basses, even amplified fiddles and banjos. Some banjo players use six-string banjos. Solo and harmony singing can be much more mellow than mountain vocalizations. Repertoires can include songs and instrumental numbers from outside country-music sources. There are people who object to such an expansive view, yet when a band sounds "Bluegrassy," there's no real reason to exclude them from the genre.

Perhaps the easiest way to think of Bluegrass is as country music's equivalent of Dixieland jazz. Against a solid or syncopated rhythm, banjo, fiddle, mandolin, and Dobro alternate solos, and, when not in the forefront, they supply countermelodies or additional rhythm. The solo-and-chorus effect is also the basis of vocalization: the lead singer is joined on choruses by two or three other singers in three- or four-part harmonies.

Bluegrass is musicians' music, a phrase best explained as "You'll appreciate it more if you play a stringed instrument a little yourself." Or even better, join others and try a Bluegrass tune. That's the way the subtleties of the music and the virtuosity of its practitioners became immediately apparent to a generation of people from both inside and outside the rural tradition. They learned that the spontaneity and effortlessness of professional groups were the result of hours of rehearsing singly and in groups to capture the exact sound that the musicians want to present. Many people delved into string-band music on a serious basis and became acquainted with its vocabulary. They learned that any instrumental piece is referred to as a "tune." A "breakdown" is a tune played at a fast tempo.* Among other terms, "old-time" (also called "old-timey") music refers to string-band music of the 1920s and 1930s, and "pickin' " means playing any instrument, not merely those whose strings are plucked—as in "How about pickin' that fiddle for us?"

They also discovered that Bluegrass is a relatively recent form. Before the early 1940s, string-band music was rough-hewn. Then through the work of Bill Monroe, a special sound began to crystalize. In one sense, it was a matter of degree: country music had always drawn elements from sources outside the hill country, and Monroe was no exception in his adding elements of blues, ragtime, and jazz. But it was also a matter of kind. Within the 2/4, 3/4, and 4/4 patterns of string-band music, Monroe taught members of his band to develop subtle flexibilities of accent and tone. Monroe's group, called the Blue Grass Boys, attracted musicians who made further contributions and refinements to the emerging

---

* One explanation of the derivation of the word "breakdown" is that the audience (and sometimes the performers) lose control when the music's pace becomes frenetic.

Roger Sprung

Wade Ward, a celebrated fiddler from North Carolina

style. Their music was an immediate success, but it took another decade before a name was applied to it. At first, people noted that other bands played "like the Blue Grass Boys," then they listened to "Bluegrass" as the band's influence made its name a generic term.

The appeal of this music takes many forms and has many reasons. Southerners know it as down-home pickin' and singin', perhaps more polished than Grandpa's fiddling or Uncle Charlie's banjo proficiency, but the same in feeling. The lyrics, whether storytelling ballads, hymns, or expressions of lost romantic or family ties, come out of the tradition of songs heard for centuries throughout the South. With respect to urban audiences, Bluegrass represents a lifestyle that is simultaneously exotic and familiar. String ties, Stetson hats, and cowboy boots worn by performers speak of the great outdoors. The music itself satisfies the same urges as wearing blue jeans, going barefoot, and joining a friendly gathering with common roots. But when a Bluegrass band launches into a breakneck number, sociological explanations sail out the window. Bluegrass is, well, just plain ol' foot-stompin', ear-to-ear grinnin', good-time music, no matter where you hail from.

TWO UP IN THE HILLS

The roots of Bluegrass go back not only in time but also in place—to the eighteenth century and Great Britain. Disgusted by what they considered to be intolerable English attempts to stop border raids, many Lowland Scots moved to Ulster, Ireland. There they found descendants of other Lowlanders who, a century before, had crossed the Irish Sea as part of an English plan to suppress the native Catholic population. However, conditions were no better. English laws against Irish manufacturing were disastrous to their important weaving industry, and in a typical display of Scots-Irish independence, they quit the British Isles for North America. Highland Scots also moved to the New World as part of a policy of dispersing clans after the Stuart revolutions of 1715 and 1745. Having little in common with New England's Puritans or the Anglicans in Tidewater, Virginia, these Calvinists traveled across the Blue Ridge Mountains and through the Cumberland Gap to the hill country of southwestern Virginia, the eastern parts of Kentucky and Tennessee, and western North and South Carolina. And along with their desire for political and social freedom, they brought their music.

Rural British music of that era was a continuation of centuries-old vocal and instrumental traditions. Ballads, which were narrative poems handed down from generation to generation, tended to be lengthy, often in excess of thirty stanzas. The longer, the better, too, for these songs were often the sole form of entertainment around a cottage hearth. The narratives chronicled a variety of subjects: historical events, supernatural occurrences, and the enduring theme of unrequited love. "Barbara Allen," the best-known ballad on both sides of the Atlantic, is an example of the last category, a tale of the "hard-hearted" lady's spurning her lover and then watching him die of a broken heart. Little if any improvisation took place, and ballads were almost always sung by a solo performer. Vocal settings for these unaccompanied songs were what musicologists call "modal," notes forming neither major nor minor scales but a combination of both (Gregorian chants and Middle Eastern music are also modal).

Instrumental music came initially from the bagpipe, and later the fiddle.* Both were adaptations of Middle Eastern instruments, first introduced in the British Isles by returning Crusaders. A piper or a fiddler was indispensable at any gathering, be it a party, a wedding, or a funeral, and he would provide accompaniment for any dancing occasion. Dances included sprightly reels, performed by sets of two, four, or eight couples, and hornpipes and jigs done without partners. According to eighteenth-century collections of fiddle music, pieces were to be played in an unembellished fashion, merely the melody without any added grace notes.

This was the musical heritage of the Scots-Irish frontiersmen who settled in Appalachian hills and hollows. Leaving psalms to New England and madrigals to Williamsburg, they perpetuated secular and rural traditions, both aspects more suitable for lives of rigor and isolation. Women rocked cradles and treadled spinning wheels to slow ballad rhythms, crooning the modal melodies in high-pitched voices. After a day's plowing, their menfolk rested fiddles in the crooks of their arms, in the old manner of playing, to scrape out "Soldier's Joy," "The Devil among the Tailors," or "Tinker's Reel." Actually, not everyone was so accomplished, and a

---

* A fiddle and a violin are physically the same, the difference coming only from the style of playing. Or, as a mountain fiddler once told his audience, "A violin ain't nothing but a fiddle with a college education."

fiddler in the family or neighborhood was a special person whose company was to be cultivated and enjoyed.

Frontiersmen were proud of their reputation as hell-raisers. It was said that "they kept the Sabbath and anything else they laid their hands on." A paucity of women meant a lack of social restraint, and gatherings of buckskin-clad hunters and trappers were sessions of drinking, fighting, and gambling. And music, too, for any fiddler within a country mile was pressed into service. Demijohns of raw corn liquor fired enthusiasms, and these self-proclaimed "half-men, half-alligators" romped and stomped until the musician was no longer able to hold his bow. Davy Crockett had a considerable reputation for playing; legend has it (at least among fiddlers) that he died at the Alamo with his rifle in one hand, his fiddle in the other.

As in any era of oral transmission of music, tunes changed. Perhaps a fiddler heard a snatch of another's playing and later tried to repeat it. If he couldn't remember the exact melody, inaccuracies or wholesale substitutions created a new piece. Just "fiddling around" also led to original compositions. New tunes and many older ones were given titles more evocative of the Appalachians than of Britain: "Cumberland Gap," "Flop Eared Mule," "Methodist Preacher," "Arkansas Traveler," and "The Old Gray Mule Came Tearing Out of the Wilderness," among countless others. A well-known tune derived from the Scottish "MacDonald's Reel," and the Irish "The Breeches On" became "Leather Breeches." (The reference was not to clothing but to food; beans dried on strings looked like pants legs and were called leather breeches.) Still known in certain areas by its original title "The King's Head," the tune "Soldier's Joy" was once called "Soldier's Pay."

Vocal music was also altered, sometimes subtly, sometimes radically. Names of characters and locales were Americanized: "The Oxford Girl" became "The Knoxville Girl," while "Bonnie George Campbell" turned into "Georgie Collins." Titles of nobility bit the dust: "Lord Randal" found himself in some parts of America as "Jimmy Randal," "Sir Lionel" became "Old Bangum." As British English became hill-country vernacular, the British version of "The Three Ravens"—

There were three ravens sat on a tree,
Down a-down, hey-down, hey-down;
There were three ravens sat on a tree,
And they were black as black might be,
With a down—

lost a bird somewhere between Scotland and Kentucky:

Two old crows sat on a tree,
Lordy, hop-di, had-di-ho;
Black and ugly as they could be,
Lordy, hop-di-had-di-ho. ✹

Violence was a perennially popular subject. Victims were shot, stabbed, drowned, poisoned, or otherwise done in, usually because of unrequited love. As in the case of "The Knoxville Girl," many lyrics were adaptations of older British ballads, while others were written to commemorate local crimes:

I started home 'twixt twelve and one,
I cried "My God, what have I done?"
I murdered the only woman I loved,
Because she would not be my bride.

And only say that you'll be mine,
In no other's arms entwined;
Down beside where the waters flow,
Down by the banks of the Ohio.

Of course, precise words, phrases, and even verses were matters of whose version one heard. Someone living even just a few miles away might sing a particular song in a completely different way, which made verse and tune swapping that much more fun.

The Appalachian region remained in a political and social vacuum throughout most of the nineteenth century, certainly until after the Civil War. Occasionally a mountaineer returning from a trip to a large town brought news of national politics, but the goings-on of pro- and antislavery movements were usually just rumors, if word reached the hills at all. Slavery was to affect these farmers later in the century, however, through black musical activities and influences. Africans had brought their own traditions to plantations, in music which touched every aspect of their work and relaxation. Whether picking cotton, chopping wood, or shucking corn, slaves sang to mark their tasks and to make time pass more quickly and easily. Pronounced rhythms marked the fall of hoes or axes, while whoever set the tempo was answered in solo-and-chorus patterns (which would later give rise to the blues form). Individuals let out mournful falsetto yelps called "hollers," answered in kind by other men working nearby.

Leisure was the time for plantation communal song and dance fests. The greater the number of people involved, the greater the number of singing, clapping, and instrumental rhythms. Instruments included drums, tambourines, pipes, and horns, all made from whatever materials were available. A 'possum skin stretched over a log became a drum; a whittled reed became a pipe or fife. As their ancestors had done in Africa, slaves attached a wooden neck to a hollowed gourd or skin-covered hoop, then added four strings to be chorded and plucked. They called it the "banjar."

Members of both races living in plantation areas often attended church services together. Contemporary accounts marveled at harmonic improvisations coming from servant pews, quite different from the music written in hymnals or played on the organ. Such singing became part of a growing tradition in which blacks would alter and embellish European music according to their own feelings about rhythm and harmony. It was not unusual for blacks to play for white dances and dancing classes, tempering their fiddling to the audience and later improvising on waltzes and minuets back in the slave quarters.

After the Civil War individuals and groups of emancipated Negroes traveled through Tennessee, Kentucky, and the western regions of Virginia and the Carolinas in search of employment. They found jobs in coal mines, in logging camps, and on railroad construction crews. Working alongside white men, they continued the practice of singing as they labored, and relaxation at a day's end would usually involve music as well. Irish railroad workers would hear their fiddling accompanied by pennywhistling and drumming as blacks who had learned the words to British ballads and urban popular songs would join in with their own brand of harmony and rhythms.

Another early example of African musical influence on European tradition took place in the form of minstrel shows. Joel Walker Sweeney, E. P. Christie, Daniel Emmett and other impresarios visited plantations to hear the singing and dancing and then formed troupes which toured northern cities. Blackface men entertained in what was called the "Ethiopian" manner: syncopated cakewalks and jigs to the beat of strummed banjos, with lyrics romanticizing the South. A classic example of minstrel-show music, "Dixie," which eventually became the Confederacy's anthem, was written by Emmett as a finale to one of his extravaganzas.

Although little of this interracial exchange had a substantial effect on Appalachian dwellers until well after the Civil War, other significant influences on mountain music had begun earlier in that century: shaped-note and religious singing. After the Revolutionary War, itinerant music teachers traveled throughout the South giving instruction in shaped-note singing. Each note's pitch was designated by a distinctive printed shape—round, square, or some form of triangle, which made learning the correct sound easier than by means of the standard ledger-line method. Singing schools were immensely popular in mountain communities, whose residents experimented in adding harmonies to ballads formerly rendered in the older monophonic style.

Harmony also marked church singing. If an area lacked a church building of its own, circuit preachers conducted prayer meetings under tents or in open air. Sacred songs were extensions of "hellfire and brimstone" sermons: joyful affirmations of God's love or lugubrious descriptions of the earthly vale of tears through which the faithful must pass en route to everlasting salvation. Most hymns were sung to New England or British compositions, although some were set to Appalachian secular melodies. The preacher would strike a tuning fork, call out the starting notes for soprano, alto, tenor, and bass parts, then lead his flock through "Amazing Grace" or "Poor Wayfaring Stranger." When there weren't enough books for all the worshipers, he might "line out" the lyrics. That involved calling out the words of the next line or two before the congregation had finished the preceding one, creating a kind of syncopation or afterbeat.*

Hymns and psalms were the only kind of music tolerated by fundamentalist sects. Children who were caught singing a "sinful" (that is, secular) ditty or, worse still, playing "the Devil's own instrument" (that is, the fiddle) were likely to receive a stern lecture, a stiff lickin', or even both. Dancing was another forbidden activity. To circumvent such restrictions, youngsters devised play-parties. "Play" referred to children's games like "Skip to My Lou" and others deemed sufficiently innocuous for teenagers and young adults, whether married or not. Singing, handclapping, and foot-

* Both shaped-note singing and lining out are still prevalent in mountain areas.

stomping provided the music for the games, which were an acceptable way of courting. Mountain girls and their beaux would alternate verses of songs like "Shady Grove":

Shady Grove, my true love,
Shady love, my darlin';
Shady Grove, my true love,
I'm goin' back to Harlan.

Wish I had a needle and thread
As fine as I could sew;
I'd sew my pretty gal to my side,
And down the road I'd go.

Verses from other songs were thrown in or strung together to another tune, thus creating an entirely new song.

More liberal sects permitted square dancing. The steps were based on certain elements of British court and country dances. As the caller directed people to "do-si-do," "allemande left," and "promenade," a fiddler provided the music. Since a set could (and often did) last for twenty or twenty-five minutes, a musician fought such boredom by singing as he played the same tune over and over. Couplets, often semi-nonsensical in content, were sung in any (or no) particular order or at any time:

Goin' up Cripple Creek, goin' in a run,
Goin' up Cripple Creek, to have a little fun;

Roll my breeches to my knees,
Wade in Cripple Creek when I please;

Goin' up Cripple Creek, find me a girl,
Sweetest little thing in the whole wide world.

His lyrics might also chronicle recent events. There was once in fact a bully named Joe Clark whose reputation increased after he chased away a stranger who had made eyes at his gal:

> *Fare thee well, Old Joe Clark,*
> *Fare thee well, I'm gone;*
> *Fare thee well, Old Joe Clark,*
> *Good-bye Betsy Brown.*

Anything which fit the meter and the fiddler's sense of whimsy was fair game:

> *I wouldn't marry the old schoolmarm,*
> *And here's the reason why:*
> *She blows her nose in stale corn bread*
> *And calls it pumpkin pie.*

Solo dancing came from one or another old-timer. When the spirit moved him, he might have leapt onto the floor and launched into a buck-and-wing or backstep. Arms akimbo, head thrown back, heels beating a staccato tattoo, he'd keep going until he collapsed. More times than not, the fiddler would become exhausted first.

As the nineteenth century drew to a close, other instruments came to erode the fiddle's exclusivity in the hill country.* It is impossible to cite with accuracy when the five-string banjo began to appear. In some areas the banjo was mentioned as early as 1870, while there are people who learned of its existence as late as the 1920s. Joe Sweeney, the minstrel-show entrepreneur, claimed to have added a fifth string to the Negro's instrument in 1832. Plucked with the thumb, the string was not fretted, its dronelike sound evoking the bagpipe to people of Scots-Irish descent. The first banjos in the Appalachians, especially ones homemade from animal skins stretched across hoops, lacked frets (the metal

---

* In point of fact, some people during the 1800s played the dulcimer, a three-stringed instrument strummed with a goose quill. Suitable for ballad accompaniment and play-parties, it was not loud enough for square-dance use.

bars across the neck.* As the player's left hand slid up to the proper note, a raggedy sound was produced. Modal tunings were used to duplicate ballad and fiddle tunes. Early playing styles included "double thumbing," whereby the right hand's thumb and index finger alternated between melody and drone notes. Another technique was called "drop thumb" (also known as "clawhammer," "knockdown," or "frailing"). A three-beat rhythm, it involved striking a melody note with the index finger's nail, rapidly followed by brushing across all five strings, then picking the fifth string with the thumb.

Guitars were frequently introduced into mountain regions by Negroes passing through and, to a lesser degree, by touring urban-based bands. Difficult to make, guitars were most often obtained through mail-order catalogues. The instrument's softer sound made it a convincing accompaniment for the sentimental ballads used in courting on a back-porch swing. In less intimate settings guitarists laid down a steady beat and chord background for fiddles and banjos.

The mandolin was the least prevalent of the four instruments, more popular in cities than in the hills. It was played either in its original Italian fashion of rapid melodic tremolos or for chorded rhythm background. Playing a gourd-shaped mandolin while standing up made a musician feel as though he were wrestling with a greased watermelon, so the flat-bucked variety was most often used. The autoharp, a pushbutton variety of zither, also came to the Appalachians through mail-order sales. Its ethereal sound lent itself to slow ballads and sacred songs more than romp-and-stomp breakdowns.

* The banjo used in Bluegrass is technologically more sophisticated. Its neck is longer than old-time "frailing" models, and the rim is made of heavy metal. To accentuate the "twanginess" and increase the instrument's volume, pickers use plastic drumheads instead of parchment or hide, and they mount a wooden or plastic resonator behind the banjo head to direct the sound forward.

This, then, was the scope and depth of Appalachian music at the turn of the present century. Its diversity could have been found even within a single family. After Grandmother sang "Barbara Allen" in her piercing, modal style, Pa would rosin the bow for a fiddle solo like "Leather Breeches" or "Leather Wing Bat." Mother might sing "Will the Circle Be Unbroken" as she had learned it at a prayer meeting, followed by the children repeating calls and couplets of a favorite square dance. Rural music was purely homegrown entertainment, and demonstrated that the past could exist alongside events that might have happened only yesterday.

THREE FIGHT INTO THE MICROPHONE

The twentieth century came to the Appalachians with the speed of a 'possum crossing a log. Dwellers in the Shenandoah Valley and Blue Ridge and Smoky Mountains first learned about the telephone and other devices through the grapevine, from neighbors who had been to large cities. But, however slowly, transportation and communication made their way through the hill country. Horses and mules bolted off the road at the sight and sound of automobiles, vehicles initially far too expensive for all but the well-to-do. Farmers, miners, and shopkeepers had to be satisfied with less luxurious artifacts of progress, and satisfied they were when someone could claim ownership of a radio or phonograph.

Eventually, thanks to mass production and lowered costs, almost every family could afford a wireless or one of Mr. Edison's talking machines. One or the other was most easily obtained through the same mail-order catalogues which were the outlets for banjos, guitars, and autoharps. Phonographs brought exotic entertainment that had never been heard in cabins or cottages. The first available records came from mail-order houses in cities and featured Irish tenors, Italian sopranos, and orchestral renditions of sentimental songs of the "When You and I Were Young, Maggie" variety. Rural music was unrecorded until 1922. That year a Texas fiddler named Eck Robertson persuaded another fiddler to go from Atlanta to New York City to make a record. They arrived at RCA Victor's studio, one wearing a cowboy outfit, the other his Confederate uniform (they had just attended a veterans' reunion). They wangled an audition, and one of Robertson's selections, "Ragtime Annie," was pressed and released as the first known recording of country music.

Realizing that a wealth of talent and material was to be found in rural areas, record companies dispatched employees and hired scouts to unearth performers. Posters and newspaper ads announced "We will pay you to sing—Horner's Hotel, 8:00 p.m., Saturday," and there would be a line of musicians at the appointed hour. The company often recorded on the spot, in another room in the hotel where equipment had been set up. (The most celebrated "find" took place in Bristol, Tennessee, in 1927 when on consecutive days the Carter Family and Jimmie Rodgers presented themselves to Ralph Peer of RCA Victor.)

But records were not the first instance of rural music's going commercial. For years every country town or hamlet was visited by medicine shows. A wagon or truck would arrive, its sign proclaiming the owner to be a "Doctor Mountebank, sole and exclusive purveyor of the celebrated Dr. Mountebank's All-Purpose Elixir." The doctor hired local musicians in advance, perhaps a banjo player and fiddler, whose playing would attract a crowd. After several minutes worth of "Sally Goodwin" or "Hell among the Yearlings," they would yield the stage to Doctor Mountebank and his sales pitch. "My elixir is guaranteed, I repeat, *guaranteed* to cure every malady from bad breath to knock-knees." The tonic, composed usually of weak tea, epsom salts, and homebrew alcohol, did have its salutary effects. The salts purged the taker while the moonshine gave him an ethereal glow, and more often than not he'd stagger back to stock up on a month's supply. One of the first things medicine-show musicians learned, however, was to insist on being paid in advance, in case dissatisfied customers ran the good doctor out of town in mid-spiel.

Grand Ole Opry

A string band appearing on *Grand Ole Opry* in the late 1940s

Early days of rural radio featured homegrown musical talent. The majority of stations broadcast only during evening hours; not only were they assured of a larger audience, but by then the announcer had finished his daytime job and the sound engineer had closed his blacksmith shop. Along with local and national news and perhaps a sermon by a circuit preacher who was passing through the area, the station would include a half hour of the local fiddling champion. After World War I, paralleling the spread of recorded rural music, several powerful (that is, 30,000 watts) stations in large cities began evening-long country-music programs. Chicago's WLS, owned by Sears Roebuck, began its *National Barn Dance* in 1924, although it featured as much popular music as country. An eighty-year-old fiddler was the first to perform on *WSM Barn Dance*, which started a year later in Nashville. Listeners applied for air time, the show achieved extraordinary popularity, and in 1926 its name was changed to *Grand Ole Opry*.

Recorded and live entertainment continued to expose hill-country people to songs that were outside their Anglo-American tradition. So did increased mobility, as folks who returned from trips to St. Louis, Memphis, New Orleans, and Atlanta spoke in glowing terms of the music they had heard along city streets. A New Orleans brass band might have reverently played "Nearer My God to Thee" as it preceded a funeral procession, breaking into a lively rendition of "Didn't He Ramble?" on the way back from the cemetery. Streetcorner guitarists wailed the blues for pennies and nickels, picking their instruments in such a way that they sounded almost like another voice. They sang of "mean, mistreatin' " women, men "doin' " and "done" wrong, and the rest of life's miseries. Jug bands were composed of men huffing and puffing across the tops of empty jugs, strumming washboards, and playing banjos and guitars. Jug-band music was heavily rhythmic (the jugs emitting an "oompa" sound), most typically in medium tempo shuffles.

Visitors to black neighborhoods at night heard Dixieland and ragtime music. Played on piano, drums, tenor banjo, and an assortment of brass and woodwinds, the music was like nothing anyone from the Appalachians had ever heard. It was marked by contrapuntal playing: when, for example, the trumpet took the lead, the trombone and clarinet played countermelodies within the chord structure. Slides and slurs produced "blue notes" as did sharps and flats played at unexpected places. A band often had a vocalist who made up blues stanzas as he or she sang. Improvisation, both vocal and instrumental, was a distinct characteristic of early twentieth century Negro music as it had been during plantation days. There was no "standard" or sacrosanct way to play any song, and such musical freedom must have appealed to more than one Appalachian traveler who returned home to experiment with blues and jazz.

The spread of recorded and broadcast music brought about

a flowering of string bands. At first, people remembered, a band was formed whenever a fiddler ran across a banjo picker. Such encounters were not infrequent during the later 1800s, especially at square dances. A banjo player usually picked individual notes on the lower strings, making countermelodies and runs to accompany the other instrument. Clawhammer-style banjo players provided a solid, steadier rhythm, particularly suitable for dance music. As guitars became more prevalent, they were used only as rhythm instruments, with chords instead of melodies played on individual strings. Mandolins, found infrequently in early string bands, were chorded as an additional rhythm source.

Eventually musicians who got together for back-porch amusement discovered that people would pay to hear them entertain. The typical way to break into show business was to approach a local radio station. In exchange for providing a bit of live entertainment, the band was permitted to announce that it was available for performances. A church social or farm group would then hire the band to play for its fund-raising activity. Dances, picnics, or box suppers would take place in a church, schoolhouse, or in someone's barn or pasture. The band was either paid a flat fee or received a percentage of the amount raised. As their reputations spread, musicians might be mentioned to a record-company scout passing through a region. If he liked their sound, out would come a recording machine, and for somewhat less than a fistful of dollars, the group would be immortalized on wax. If the band didn't have a name, that matter was often solved on the spot. Counties and states figured prominently, as in the Leake County Revelers and the North Carolina Ramblers. Groups gave the impression of being carefree country folk, and leaders or reasonably well-known members had their names attached: Earl Johnson's Clodhoppers, Doctor Smith's Champion Horsehair Pullers, and Fiddlin' John Carson's Virginia Reelers.

Fiddlin' John had been the first rural performer to be re-

corded by RCA Victor's Ralph Peer. Whether playing alone
or with his band, Carson's successes demonstrated that hill
people were more than willing to buy records which some
city-based record company executives characterized as corny.
His records contained dazzling fiddle playing and were pure
entertainment, for he regarded a microphone as he did any
barn-dance audience. Carson began the old hoedown "Dance
All Night with a Bottle in Your Hand" with "Now I'm gonna
play you a tune entitled 'You Can't Get Milk from a Cow
Named Ben.' " Buyers lapped it up.

Within a year of Carson's first recording, a Georgia chicken
farmer named Gid Tanner formed a band he called the Skillet Lickers. Tanner played fiddle, accompanied by the blind
guitarist Riley Puckett, Clayton McMitchen on second fiddle,
and Fate Norris on banjo. Theirs was a wild and woolly
sound; after a spoken introduction such as "Here we are
again, grab your gal and dance!" they launched into breakdowns at hell-for-leather speeds. Like square-dance musicians, they interspersed couplets somewhere in certain
tunes:

> Dog in a rye field, dog in a holler,
> Bring him back, boy, and I'll give you a dollar.

The repertoire of the Skillet Lickers reflected what a mixed
bag of sources string bands had been using. They recorded
sentimental ballads like "Let Me Call You Sweetheart" and
Negro-originated songs such as "John Henry." Riley Puckett's guitar work was particularly suited for blues; his bass
runs in double or quadruple time were almost melodies in
themselves.

Less boisterous in sound was Charlie Poole and his North
Carolina Ramblers. The band was one of the first to earn
enough money from its music to allow its members to become full-time entertainers (unlike others who had to keep
their jobs in mills, factories, and on farms). Its success was

well deserved, for Poole was an excellent banjo player. His three-finger style produced more than just rhythmic accompaniment for fiddlers—it picked out discernible though ragged melodies. The Ramblers' most popular record, "Don't Let Your Deal Go Down," was musically slightly more sophisticated than most mountain tunes; it consisted of ragtimelike progressions of fifth chords rather than the usual tonic, subdominant, and dominant chords.* Their singing, however, like that of other bands, remained a product of the hill country. Intonations and nasal timbre were not much different from the unaccompanied modal ballads still sung at that time.

The Depression caused many musicians to lose their full-time jobs, and it brought an end to much of the preceding decade's string-band music. Money, especially for entertainment, was as scarce in the Appalachians as anywhere else in the country, and fifty cents or one dollar to buy a record was too much for most people. Recording companies cut back on new releases, and rural groups were among the first to go. Those radio stations that could afford to stay in business after losing advertising revenue played more contemporary music, as exotic as possible to help relieve "hard times." One of the most exotic forms, especially to people of Anglo-American heritage, came from Hawaii. Bands from the Islands had been touring the mainland during the twenties and thirties and were featured on many radio programs. High-pitched melodies sliding out of steel guitars caught the fancy of rural guitarists who raised the bridges of their instruments and fretted the strings with metal bars to produce the effect.† The Dopera brothers, Czechoslavakian immigrants, manufactured a raised-bridge guitar in the 1920s. A metal resonator in

---

* That's technical talk for, in the key of C, a C–E–A–G–C progression, as opposed to series of just C, F, and G chords.
† Some Negro bluesmen had been fretting their guitars with a knife blade or bottle neck to obtain the same sound, but their ingenuity was little known in the hill country.

the instrument's body amplified the slides and whines produced by fretting the metal strings with a steel bar. Like the
steel guitar (but unlike acoustic guitars), the instrument was
not chorded; melodies and runs came from picking strings
which were tuned to an open chord. The brothers named
their product the Dobro (a Slavic word meaning "good") and,
through mail-order sales and swapping, the instrument made
its way along the Appalachian mountain chain.

The adjectives "smoother" and "livelier" characterize rural
music of the middle and late 1930s. Not that older gospel
songs lacked harmonic fluidity or that traditional fiddle tunes
had not been played fast enough to beat a hound to a raccoon,
but the music now had a different feeling. Jazzy syncopation
and improvisation began to eclipse modal singing and strict
melodic playing. Accordingly, older mountain styles fell into
disuse. Banjos gathered dust as people turned to other instruments. Although the tenor banjo remained in Dixieland
and ragtime bands, a five-string was rarely heard on *Grand
Ole Opry* or the other barn-dance shows, and when it did
show up it was usually in the hands of a baggy-pants "hayseed" comedian.

Radio and record listeners who liked traditional mountain
ballads could occasionally find them in the repertoires of
duet acts. Because there was a quality about close fraternal
harmonies that audiences found particularly appealing,
brother acts were recorded and promoted all over the South.
Mandolins or steel guitars took the melody part which had
formerly been the fiddle's bailiwick. One of the most important brother groups, Rabon and Alton Delmore, had a Negro-
influenced blues and ragtime sound. Cliff and Bill Carlisle
featured Cliff's virtuoso Dobro and steel guitar work. Homer
and Walter Callahan performed many older ballads as well as
a version of "The House of the Rising Sun." Bill and Earl
Bolick, better known as the Blue Sky Boys, were a guitar and
mandolin duet. They too sang such sentimental Anglo-

Buck "Uncle Josh" Graves tuning his Dobro guitar

American ballads as "The Butcher Boy," "Mary of the Wild Moor," and "The Knoxville Girl," as well as religious songs. Very few happy lyrics came from the Blue Sky Boys; they reflected a preoccupation with dying parents, unrequited love, and a fundamentalist view of life's woes.

The McGhee Brothers, Sam and Kirk, had a rougher, more insistent sound. They toured with Uncle Dave Macon as part of Grand Ole Opry shows, their guitar and banjo forming a part of Uncle Dave's Fruit Jar Drinkers. In 1930 they joined "Fiddlin' " Arthur Smith as the Dixieliners. Smith is often cited as the most influential fiddler in country music. His shuffle and roll bowing and his manner of sliding into and away from notes was an important precursor of contemporary Bluegrass fiddling.

Other kinds of country music had an influence on hill-country musicians growing up in the 1930s. From Texas and Oklahoma came Western swing, a combination of popular big-band, Mexican, and traditional mountain styles. When a band such as the Texas Playboys or the Light Crust Dough-boys did "Old Joe Clark," the melody might have sounded like the square-dance breakdown, but "hot" fiddling, a jazzy brass section, and solid drumming made it a whole new breed of cat. The blues and yodeling of Jimmie Rodgers were familiar to everyone who had a radio or phonograph. In a more traditional style, the Carter Family had a profound impact in their close harmonic arrangements of mountain ballads. Mother Maybelle Carter's guitar playing was a distinctive feature; in a style learned from black musicians, she picked out melodies on bass strings while strumming chords.

All of this is not to say that there was no string-band music even during the Depression days. On an individual basis, fiddlers continued to compete at fiddlers' conventions. Entrants generally chose their own tunes, although sometimes they were asked to play a hornpipe, polka, or a waltz. The applause of the audience determined the winner, and it was not

Grand Ole Opry

A string band posing for a publicity photograph

always just the music that made them favor one musician over the rest. Clayton McMitchen would spend hours applying rosin to his bow, so that when he bore down during "Fire on the Mountain," clouds of powder caused audiences to gasp and yell "His fiddle's on fire!" Curly Fox played so hard that horsehair snapped and flew away from his bow. Then there were the times when a youngster would be pushed shyly onto the stage, only to bring home the bacon with a performance which left his elders gaping.

The five-string banjo was still going strong in the western part of North Carolina. Its foremost practitioner in the 1930s was Snuffy Jenkins, whose three-finger style was to influence every banjo player who heard him. Jenkins played "rolls," series of three or four notes based on chords that when linked together made smoother, more melodic patterns than Charlie Poole had been producing. Wade Mainer was another banjo picker from that part of the state; he belonged to a band headed by one of his brothers, J. E. Mainer's Mountaineers. This was a large group by string-band standards, including fiddle, banjo, mandolin, guitar, and string bass, and headed by J. E. Mainer, one of the most popular fiddlers of the decade. At the age of fifteen, J.E. had gone to Knoxville to find a job. As he got off the train, he heard a fiddler who was leaning against a telephone pole and playing "Drunkard's Hiccups," an appropriate selection, for the musician had obviously been drinking heavily. When he finished the tune, the fiddler staggered across the tracks and was hit by a passing train. J.E. returned later that day, found the fiddle (which had been knocked across the railroad yard into a patch of high grass), and so acquired his first instrument. Although he played many tunes in the "blues fiddle" style, the Mountaineers were best known for zesty, ebullient renditions of mountain tunes like "Train 45," "Wild Bill Jones," and "Run Mountain." The band's name for a while was "The Crazy Mountaineers," in honor of its sponsor, not its sanity. They had been hired in 1934 by the Crazy Water Crystals Company, one of the growing number of groups to become associated with commercial interests. (Another group, Fisher Hendley and the Aristocratic Pigs, was sponsored by a pork-processing concern.)

Still another band working out of the same area of North Carolina was the Morris Brothers. Zeke Morris (who had played mandolin with Wade Mainer's Sons of the Mountaineers) and his brother Wiley recorded several mandolin and guitar duets, including their own composition "Salty Dog." They added other musicians in 1938, including (at different times) banjo players Earl Scruggs and Don Reno. Compared to the Mountaineers, the Morris Brothers' band had a more "refined" sound, with smoother quartet vocal harmonies and more controlled instrumental playing.

Many string bands were as adept at comedy as they were at music. Stage appearances involved members in blackface, in the tradition of nineteenth-century minstrel shows. Their humor was unabashedly and intentionally corny, especially when it was of the "Arkansas Traveler" putting-down-the-city-slicker dialogue:

How'd your taters turn out?
They didn't turn out, me and Sal had to dig 'em out!

Ain't much distance 'tween you and a fool.
Only this microphone.

Skits done over radio often required the presence of a sound-effects man, who frantically slammed doors, honked horns, or made porcine grunts at the signals of the director.

Between the World Wars, mountain music had become smooth, jazzy, and commercial. Some old-timers shook their heads with dismay at the way singing and instrumental styles of their ancestors had been tampered with, but they were in the minority. Through records and radio, diverse musical elements had inundated the mountains, and at every confluence the resulting streams gathered greater force as they came down from the hills.

FOUR BILL MONROE AND THE BLUE GRASS BOYS

One of the many brother duets that flourished during the 1930s was Bill and Charlie Monroe. They did as well, if not better, than most, and their excellent record sales and packed personal appearances attested to their close vocal harmonies and dynamic guitar and mandolin work. But the name Monroe—Bill Monroe—deserves far more than a passing mention or even several paragraphs. Quite simply, if it had not been for Bill Monroe, there might never have been Bluegrass music at all.

The youngest of eight children, Bill Monroe was born in 1911 near the town of Rosine in western Kentucky. His family was of Anglo-American stock, descended from President James Monroe. Although the music that had been transplanted from the British Isles was the family's living heritage, there had been a considerable influence from black musical traditions. Western Kentucky was an area where many Negroes had passed through or settled, and an interaction of black and white music was an accepted and acceptable part of life. A case in point was Arnold Schultz, a black fiddler and guitar player. His virtuosity was legendary, and people would travel for miles to hear him play for square dancing. Bill Monroe, himself a guitarist from the age of twelve, was particularly impressed by Schultz's smooth transitions between chords, as well as his blues playing, which is not surprising when one compares the raw tonalities of Negro blues and the "lonesome" sound of mountain modal ballads and fiddle tunes. Monroe often accompanied

Schultz's fiddling at dances, listening to and assimilating his sound.

Another of Bill's idols was his mother's brother, Pennoyer Vanderver. Crippled in an accident, Vanderver needed help on his farm, and Bill was a willing volunteer. Uncle Pen was the best fiddler in the region and took his nephew along when he played for dances. The boy learned a great deal about the subtleties of tone and bow timing even in such often-heard tunes as "Turkey in the Straw" and "Soldier's Joy." After his parents died, Bill lived with his uncle. Days were filled with hard, hot work, but an evening's relaxation with Uncle Pen and his fiddle were among the best times that Monroe remembers.

As so many other Southerners had been forced to do, Bill's brothers Charlie and Birch went north to find employment, no mean accomplishment at a time when the Depression was beginning to close its grip over the nation. Bill followed them in 1928, to a suburb of Chicago where he got a job loading oil barrels. Then, in 1932, a radio station came to the rescue. The *WLS Barn Dance* sent out a road company to perform at places within its broadcasting range. The troupe included a set of square dancers, and the Monroe brothers were part of the act. Touring for more money than heavy labor would have earned them, Bill, Charlie, and Birch played at every opportunity. Bill became intrigued with the notion of becoming a professional musician. His first choice was the fiddle, but since Birch had already selected that instrument, Bill settled on the mandolin.

With the sounds of Arnold Schultz and Uncle Pen Vanderver indelibly imprinted in his memory, Monroe set about applying fiddle techniques to the mandolin. The mandolin had hitherto been used to produce either chorded rhythms or plinky Italianate melodies. Monroe, however, saw it as a vibrant, decisive lead instrument. Tuned as a fiddle, it had the potential for bluesy slides and accents like its bowed cousin. Monroe worked on developing additional dimensions: single notes strained into whining blues notes, sharp sustained tremolos, and bouncy rhythms.

When Birch decided not to pursue a professional musician's career, Bill and Charlie worked on duet numbers. They found a sponsor in the Texas Crystal Company and appeared on a local Saturday evening radio program. By the time they moved to South Carolina in 1937, the Monroe Brothers had become country-music celebrities. Their repertoire consisted of traditional mountain murder ballads, such as "Banks of the Ohio," sentimental songs, and religious numbers, including "Mother's Not Dead (She's Only A Sleeping)," and "The Great Speckled Bird." At the peak of their success, the brothers developed some differences of opinion. Bill felt he was still being treated like a kid brother, even though he was making substantial contributions to the music, and he also wanted to work for a fuller sound. He did not merely contemplate a string band, but a full group of musicians that could tap the kinds of rural music then so popular: Carter Family harmonies and instrumentals, Jimmie Rodgers' yodeling blues, Western swing, and Dixieland jazz and ragtime.

The brothers separated * and Bill formed his first band in 1938. The lead singer and guitar player was Cleo Davis, with Art Wooten on fiddle, John Miller on jug, and Amos Garen on bass fiddle. Monroe called them the Blue Grass Boys, after the nickname of his native state.† He worked hard to achieve the sound he heard in his mind's ear: hard-driving and tight playing and singing, combining elements of brother

---

* Charlie went on to establish his own group, the Kentucky Partners. The band's lack of banjo and inclusion of electric guitar made it a country-music group, not a Bluegrass band, similar to Roy Acuff's Smoky Mountain Boys. He retired from professional music in 1955.

† A digression: Consider, if Monroe had been born in a neighboring mountain state, would this book's subtitle have been "The Story of Volunteer Music" (for Tennessee), ". . . Tarheel . . ." (North Carolina), ". . . Old Dominion . . ." (Virginia), or even ". . . Palmetto . . ." (South Carolina)?

Clark Thomas

Bill Monroe

duets, fiddle breakdowns, church harmonies, and jazz. The Blue Grass Boys soon made people who had thought string bands were a thing of the past sit up and take notice. Their immediate popularity won them bookings on *Grand Ole Opry* in 1939. Under the aegis of the program, the Blue Grass Boys toured the South, and eventually signed with RCA Victor Records. The recordings increased Monroe's following, and old mountain tunes and country blues took on new significance with his high piercing vocal harmonies and distinctive mandolin playing. An addition to the band during this period was comedian and banjo player Dave Akeman, better known to *Opry* audiences as "Stringbean." Stringbean's clawhammer banjo style added yet another rhythm instrument. (At RCA's suggestion, Monroe had experimented briefly with an accordion and an electric guitar but later rejected them.)

Although he continued to appear on the *Opry*, Monroe decided to establish his own touring company in 1941. He had no difficulty persuading several other popular entertainers to join his troupe: the Negro harmonica player De-Ford Bailey, the banjo player-singer-comedian Uncle Dave Macon, and the old-timey string bandsmen Sam and Kirk McGee. The shows were wholesome family fare, performed under a large tent with portable bleacher seats and a sound and light system. Young musicians from all over the South polished their techniques to emulate the style of the Blue Grass Boys, with the hope that maybe, if they were good, they'd be asked to join the band someday.

Three other men joined the group by 1945, and the nature of Monroe's music changed even more. In singer-guitarist Lester Flatt, Monroe found a lead voice that blended with his own high tenor for soaring harmonies. Several months later Earl Scruggs became one of the Blue Grass Boys. His three-finger style did for the banjo what Monroe's innovations had done for the mandolin: he turned it into a lead instrument. The third person was Chubby Wise, a fiddler whose playing had much of the same bluesy sound as Monroe's mandolin work.

Many people point to these men as the finest in the band's history. With Cedric Rainwater (real name: Howard Watts) on bass fiddle, the sound of the Blue Grass Boys began to take shape and crystalize. When Scruggs was not taking a solo break, he played countermelodic patterns high on the banjo's neck. Chubby Wise was equally adept at bluesy "soulful" tones as he was lining out the tune of traditional fiddle pieces. Like Howdy Forrester and Tommy Magness, his predecessors in the band, Wise used double-stop techniques for a fuller sound. (The occasional addition of another fiddle or even as many as three of them gave certain tunes a strong bagpipe quality.) Lester Flatt's open-chorded guitaring supplied both melodic runs and a pervasive rhythm. And

of course there was Monroe's mandolin, floating like a butter-
fly on some notes, then stinging like a bee to urge the band's
beat ahead. Almost every number they did became something of a standard, whether it was an instrumental designed
to display individual virtuosity, a gospel song featuring trio
or quartet singing, or one of Monroe's original compositions,
like "Footprints in the Snow," "Muleskinner Blues" (based
on Jimmie Rodgers' "Blue Yodel #8"), or "Molly and Tenbrooks" (the last telling the story of an 1878 horse race between the Eastern Thoroughbred champion Ten Brook and
Molly, a challenger from California).*

Monroe brought a new kind of dignity to his variety of
country music. He took it away from baggy-pants outhouse
and slapstick comedy. The Blue Grass Boys wore broad-
brimmed hats, high riding boots, and breeches, like members
of a cavalry remount platoon. Later, as the cowboy mystique
made rural music known as country-and-western, the band
appeared in Stetson hats and string ties. Never flamboyant,
they looked like respectable and respectful guests on someone's stage.

To be a member of the Blue Grass Boys was physically and
emotionally demanding, since the band seemed always to be
on the road. Consecutive appearances might be four hundred
miles apart, or as much as a thousand, and the distances had
to be covered by a nonstop drive. As band members learned,
it was possible to be booked into two theaters in the same
town on the same afternoon. "Bicycling" was the term for
racing between the two theaters, first appearing between
showings of a movie and then leaving for another theater
before the applause had died down.

Bill Monroe himself was also demanding. He lived and
breathed his kind of music. He knew what he wanted, and

* Monroe's songs influenced other musicians. In 1950 Pee Wee King was inspired by
Monroe's "Kentucky Waltz" to write perhaps the nation's best-known country song,
"Tennessee Waltz."

expected the highest degree of cooperation from his men. No shortcuts, no fudging, nothing but honest picking and singing. That was what had established the band's reputation, what audiences were paying good money to hear. Perhaps more important, however, it was what Monroe wanted to hear. Standing to one side while another player took a solo, he would cock his head to the side as if assessing whether the music met his high standards.

Scruggs left the band in 1948, to be replaced by Don Reno. Flatt left several months later, succeeded by Jim Eanes, and later by Mac Wiseman. As in any fraternity, newcomers were initiated by practical jokes such as the one Reno recalls:

We were driving through eastern Kentucky one night. It might have been through the town of Hazard. Bill pulled over to the side of the road and announced we were lost. I was new with the band, so he asked me to knock on a farmhouse door and ask where we were. Of course Bill knew we weren't lost and that the place belonged to a moonshiner. Anyway, I knocked on the door, and when it opened I found myself staring down the barrel of a shotgun. You just don't go knockin' on moonshiners' doors. The guy asked "What you want, boy?" I stammered something about playing banjo with Bill Monroe and that we were lost. The guy looked at me kind of funny. "Lost? That son-of-a-bitch ain't lost. Are you sure you play banjo with Bill Monroe? Where's he at?" "Up on the road," I told him. "You just call him," the man told me; "stay right where you are and call him." So I yelled "Bill! Bill!" Bill came on down; he thought it was the funniest thing he ever saw. He and the moonshiner had a good laugh on the joke.

Recreation came most frequently in the form of baseball, for a bat and ball were two of Monroe's few acceptable substitutes for rosin and fingerpicks. The Blue Grass Boys and their touring associates were expected to play ball, sometimes against local teams and other times against a squad formed within the group. Although Monroe won't actually admit to having employed ringers, two members of his troupe who were less than breathtaking musicians had once

Steve Arkin

Bill Monroe with the Blue Grass Boys in 1973

played professional ball. After nine innings, it was time to grab the instruments and perform, and then to hit the road again. At first, transportation was supplied by touring cars (including a Packard limousine of considerable vintage), which were later superseded by buses. Don Reno remembers Monroe's first bus, which had seen service on a city route in Florida:

Bill bought it during the summer and kept putting off installing a heater. We were in Nebraska during that winter and the temperature was well below zero. Joel Price, who was our bass player, had a habit of taking so much Bromo Seltzer that we took to calling him "Bromo." He and I were lying on mattresses in the back of the bus trying to keep warm. Joel wanted a dose of Bromo, so he reached over for a jar of water that he always carried and poured the powder into it. Well, he took a swig and jumped up screaming. The water had frozen over, and Joel got a mouthful of powder. He looked like he was foaming at the mouth. Later that night we got a kerosene heater and I burned my coattails on it trying to keep warm. What a bus! Everybody tried to think up ways to blow up the engine so we wouldn't have to ride in it anymore.

Scruggs, Flatt, Wiseman, and Reno were among the first in a procession of musicians associated with the Blue Grass Boys who left to form or join other bands. To mention everyone who played in the band would require an endless list, resembling the lists of Biblical "begats," but some of the best known were singers-guitarists Jimmy Martin, Jim Eanes, and Carter Stanley, fiddlers Vassar Clements and Bobby Hicks, and banjo players Sonny Osborne, Bill Keith, and Vic Jordan. To use a baseball metaphor, the Blue Grass Boys were the New York Yankees of the Ruth-Gehrig and Mantle-Maris eras. Every audience was certain to include at least one youngster carrying an instrument, eager for a tryout (like the kids who take their mitts to a major-league game). Monroe would tell some to come back in a year or two, while others were signed up immediately, depending on vacancies and proficiency. There was never a dearth of talent, and the band always managed to come up with a glittering all-star lineup.

But the days of living high off the hog began to wane sometime around 1956 or 1957. Country music found itself in trouble, and the reason was rock 'n' roll. Although its roots included hillbilly and country blues, rock 'n' roll was quite different from traditional mountain music. Elvis Presley sang Monroe's "Blue Moon of Kentucky" on the flip side of his first single, but it didn't sound anything like the original. That was the problem for Monroe and other traditional performers: much rock 'n' roll was flamboyant, brash, and loud. Some country singers made the transition easily; Sonny James and Marty Robbins are two examples. Others were eclipsed by rock 'n' roll, and Monroe was one of them. Not that he had a necessary aversion to amplification (after all he had included an electric guitar on some of his earlier recordings of Jimmie Rodgers' songs), yet to go "modern" was something of an ideological surrender. Whereas string bands had suffered during the Depression because audiences lacked money, they were equally affected by affluence two decades later. Disc jockeys rode roughshod over traditional country music in favor of the sounds that appealed to teenagers and their ample allowances. However, Monroe would not entertain the idea of compromise. Let others add drums or electric guitars and basses and let them sing Chuck Berry or Chubby Checkers hits—that wasn't his line of country. And so it was a rough period for Monroe. He had difficulty attracting and retaining musicians of the caliber he was used to, for the money was elsewhere. The Blue Grass Boys continued to perform, but not to the extent of former nonstop bookings.

If rock 'n' roll had overwhelmed the South like Sherman's march to the sea, salvation, or at least substantial aid, soon followed. Interest in folk music had been building up in coffee houses and campuses across the country. Students began to listen to Pete Seeger, the Weavers, Joan Baez, and the Kingston Trio. When playing a guitar or banjo became fashionable, many youngsters went beyond three or four basic chords to discover the real creators and perpetuators of ballads and tunes. Northern folk festivals tried to offer a representative sampling of traditional rural music, and students of folklore were quick to recommend the Blue Grass Boys. Monroe and the Boys were soon knocking 'em dead at Newport, Philadelphia, and other places. Hearing the music live was a catalyst for even more people to investigate rural musical styles more deeply. Life looked up for Monroe as he once again had a full complement of bookings. His band drove between urban areas and rural fairs, since few promoters failed to include the Blue Grass Boys.

Like their country counterparts, many men from cities became extraordinarily proficient and inventive in older mountain styles of playing. Bill Keith was one. Born in Philadelphia and educated at Amherst College, Keith gravitated toward a banjo technique that produced melodies from single notes perfectly. The technique involved playing exact melody notes as one would on a fiddle, including half-step "chromatics" similar to slides and slurs. Rather than strike the same string twice in a row, Keith worked out tunes on successive strings. Suppose, for example, a melody moved from G to A to C sharp to D. Instead of playing an open third string (for the G), then the same string up two frets (for the A), followed by the second string up two (for the C sharp), and the same string on the third fret (for the D), Keith would play the open third string (the G), then the fourth string fretted at the seventh fret (for the A), the second string at the second fret (for the C sharp), followed by the open first string (sounding the D). The result was a clear, rapidly produced melody without any of the approximation to which Scruggs-style picking was occasionally confined. Although "Keith-style" playing was unlike anything Monroe had heard, the new sound appealed to him, and Keith joined the band. Other members of the Blue Grass Boys who came from outside usual string-band country included Richard Greene, Pete Rowan, and Gene Lowinger. (Those who wore their hair long were instructed to tuck it under their cowboy hats during performances.)

One such Northerner was Steve Arkin, who spent a summer vacation from school playing banjo with the Blue Grass Boys. Since the dream of any Bluegrass musician has its occasional disillusionments, at one point he considered leaving the band, and, lacking the money to return home, telephoned his parents to request the necessary funds. The place was Livonia, Georgia, and the time was the summer of 1963, when civil-rights workers were being harassed and worse throughout the South.

I phoned from a gas station where a group of the local gentry was lounging around. When the men heard me ask the operator to place a call to Brooklyn, New York, they moved toward me with blood in their eyes. Just then, my mother got on the line. "Hi, Mom," I yelled into the receiver; "I sure am having a good time picking banjo for *Bill Monroe* and the *Blue Grass Boys!*" When I finished my call, one of the locals looked me over and asked dubiously, "You're a Yankee and you can pick a five?" I admitted that I was and I could. He continued, "You sure you're not down here to inter-fere with our way of life?" I assured the fellow that that was the fur-thest thought from my mind and that I was there only as a member of the Blue Grass Boys.

The men remained skeptical. "Where's Bill Monroe at?" one asked and then suggested that we all take a walk to see him. So with me leading the parade, we went down the street to where Bill was standing beside the bus. Apparently satisfied that they were indeed talking to Mr. Bill Monroe, one of the men commented that "This Yankee says he can pick the five." My anxiety was considerably re-lieved by Bill's laconic confirmation, "I believe he can."

Another episode provided Arkin with more discomfort than danger.

We were going from Nashville to play a date in Fredericks, Mary-land. The bus broke down at about three in the morning, some-where near Charlottesville. No one could fix whatever was wrong and we all went back to sleep. By the dawn's early light we discov-ered that we had stopped right in front of a garage owned by Don Reno. We ended up leaving the bus there and borrowing a '47 Ford. Although Bill is a conservative driver and passenger, his maxim that "The Blue Grass Boys are *never* late" prevailed and he instructed the driver to get us to Fredericks with all due haste. What a ride! Ninety miles an hour at some points in a car with no shock ab-sorbers. And no rest stops—"The Blue Grass Boys are *never* late." Then it began to rain and we arrived (on time, of course) to face a downpour. But since the band wouldn't be paid unless it performed, Bill led us on the stage and we did an entire show. It didn't matter that there was absolutely no one in the audience or that the stage had no roof.

The trip back was no better. The Ford gave out in the middle of the night, no one would stop to pick us up, and when we tried to use the phone at a nearby house, we were turned away. Somehow we got word to Reno, who sent his son to get us. Bill wouldn't get into Ronnie's souped-up car, so another fellow and I went back to fetch the bus. The Ford, the ride, the performance, and the trip back—the whole experience was out of a surrealistic movie.

Another member of the band was James Monroe, Bill's son. James has been a Bluegrass picker (lead singer and guitar) since the early sixties. He joined his father's band, receiving baptism under fire at important concerts and festivals until he formed his own group, the Midnight Ramblers.

Like his music, Bill Monroe has endured. His band's name has become the generic term for his kind of music. Monroe considers his band to be an ongoing training ground, for to be a member is to carry on its spirit as much as its sound. Two recent episodes reflect this feeling. Every autumn Grand Ole Opry presents a Bluegrass concert as part of an annual country-music disc jockeys' convention held in Nashville. The cast includes Lester Flatt, Jimmy Martin, Don Reno, and Mac Wiseman, each first appearing with his own band, then joining Monroe to do the songs they did when they were with the Blue Grass Boys. Those who accuse Monroe of having lost his verve may have sober second thoughts when they see Lester Flatt or Jimmy Martin sidle up and sing; everyone responds like race horses hearing the call to the post, with the same drive and energy that they showed when they were members of his band. Finally everyone on the show comes out on stage, the cast of characters including many other Blue Grass Boys alumni. They all pick away in a ripsnorting finale, a Tabernacle Choir of Bluegrass.

One need not be a professional to play with Monroe. Of late he has invited "parking lot pickers" to join his band at the conclusion of his concerts. As instruments pop out of cases during intermission, a stageful of people shuffle alongside the Blue Grass Boys. A dozen or so guitars slap out the chords to "Sally Goodwin" or "Cripple Creek" while fiddles and banjos dive into the melody, tentatively at first, then more emphatically. A pint-size mandolin player is urged into the spotlight, his body shaking harder than his pick. Monroe tempers his playing to accommodate the youngster's hesitancy, speeding up when he senses the boy's capability. For a while they match each other note-for-note, Monroe launching into instrumental harmonies at certain places. Then a banjo picker, perhaps the area's Bluegrass fair-haired boy, takes the lead. Monroe listens approvingly, nodding at the man's sense of timing. A glance toward his band is the signal that it's time for the ensemble to bring it all back home. Everyone backpedals over the final notes and chords, the hall reverberating into something akin to a glorious "Amen." And no wonder. After all, everyone involved knows he has been playing with the Father of Bluegrass.

FIVE LESTER FLATT AND EARL SCRUGGS AND THE FOGGY MOUNTAIN BOYS

Shake any tree in North Carolina, it is said, and a banjo picker will fall out. With that kind of Tarheel attachment to the instrument, it is more than fitting that someone from the state has become synonymous with the five-string. That man is Earl Scruggs, whose contributions in both technique and influence have earned him a front-and-center place in the Bluegrass spotlight.

Earl Scruggs was born in 1924 in Flint Hill, a town in the western part of North Carolina. There was no shortage of fine banjo pickers, whether heard over the radio, on a neighbor's back porch, or in the family farmhouse. Growing up in such an atmosphere, Earl started to play at an early age: when at the age of six he was so impressed with a blind musician's rendition of "Home Sweet Home," he had already been a veteran picker for two years. Sometimes Earl played a small instrument owned by his cousin Smith Hammett, but when he used his brother's full-sized five-string, Earl was obliged to rest its head on the floor or a nearby chair. Any banjo that found its way into the youngster's hands was in constant use. One day, at the age of eleven, he was pouting about something and taking out his feelings on the banjo. The tune was "Reuben," and Earl noticed that the melody was coming out in a particularly smooth fashion. Glancing down at his right hand, he saw that he was doing more than double-thumbing.

Although often credited with having invented three-finger picking, Scruggs is quick to acknowledge that others had greased the path. Going beyond the two-finger style

then so prevalent in string bands, Smith Hammett and Snuffy
Jenkins were well-known in North Carolina for their technique
of using their middle fingers in addition to thumb and index
finger. Earl's brothers Junie and Horace learned that style,
and Earl picked it up from them. But if he was not the origi-
nator, Scruggs did contribute a good deal toward the refine-
ment of the technique.* The basis of Scruggs' style was a
series of rolls, those arpeggio patterns of connected notes that
had distinguished Jenkins' playing. But rather than simply
playing a series of rolls, Scruggs added "drone" notes, extra
notes within a chord. The result was unbroken streams of
melody surrounded by cascades of grace notes. As older clawhammer pickers had done, he used his left hand to slide
through, hammer on, and pull off additional notes. Sharper,
bouncing notes came from "pinching," or simultaneously
plucking two strings.

An elementary lesson in Scruggs-picking may clarify matters. According to banjo tablature, strings are numbered one
through five, beginning with the bottom string as the instrument is held. For example, in an open-G chord (gDGBD),
the G string is designated the third and the B is the second
string. Right-hand fingers are marked T, I, and M, for thumb,
index, and middle finger, respectively.

A basic roll is "3–1–5–3–1–5–3–1," written in tablature as
3/I, 1/M, 5/T, 3/I, 1/M, 5/T, 3/I, 1/M. Another is 3/T, 2/I, 1/M,
5/T, which requires the thumb to alternate between the third
and fifth strings (as in older-style "double-thumbing"). All of
this is easily manageable at slow speeds, but when one plays
at a breakneck tempo and tries to work out melody notes
within these rolls, getting the correct finger at the right place
at the right time is something like juggling five balls at once,
at least for a novice picker.

Young Scruggs' innovations earned him a considerable rep-

---

* For a somewhat dissenting view of Scruggs' landmark position, see Don Reno's comments in Chapter Six.

utation around Flint Hill. When he played at fiddlers' conventions, the three-dollar first prize given to winners of banjo competitions more than compensated for the long hikes there and back. But music remained an avocation. As a teenager, Scruggs worked in a textile mill and put in long hours, which so affected his health that he was rejected for military service when World War II began. Forced to leave mill work for reasons of health, Scruggs spent the early 1940s as a member of various bands. Carrying a box of jams and jellies provided by his mother, he went to South Carolina in 1941 to succeed Don Reno with the Morris Brothers on their early-morning radio program (the three-finger picking gave the band a sound which many call the first true Bluegrass). 1945 found him a member of Lost John Miller and the Allied Kentuckians. Based in Knoxville, Tennessee, the band traveled to Nashville for an early-morning radio program every Saturday. One Saturday the Blue Grass Boys were also in Nashville for a stint on *Grand Ole Opry,* and Jimmy Shumate, the group's fiddler, urged Scruggs to join Monroe's organization. Scruggs was reluctant. He did not want to leave Miller, nor was he sure how Monroe would feel about his style (at that time the Blue Grass Boys used a tenor banjo for rhythm). But when Lost John disbanded the Kentuckians, Scruggs asked Shumate whether he could arrange an audition after all. And so it happened that on a Saturday afternoon, Monroe asked Scruggs to join the band for that evening's *Opry* performance, and Scruggs finally became a member of the Blue Grass Boys.

If Monroe's group had caused audiences to sit up and take notice before that time, the addition of Scruggs created an even greater impact. Along with the mandolin and fiddle, Scruggs' banjo was a lead instrument which increased the band's versatility and repertoire, as his fingers snapped out twangy fusillades of staccato notes on breakdown solos. During sentimental ballads and hymns, his improvisational patterns in the banjo's higher registers added almost another voice to vocals. His nonstop rolls were also perfect for filling in gaps between vocal lines with eight- or ten-note phrases.

Thanks to Scruggs, the five-string pulled the greatest revival act since Lazarus. Men who would later become professional musicians listened to the Blue Grass Boys and were inspired to try their hands. Bobby Osborne, for one, heard one *Opry* show and decided that the banjo part on "Cumberland Gap" was like nothing that ever came through a radio. Don Stover recalls being stymied until someone informed him that Scruggs used three fingers, not just two. When he learned that metal finger picks wrapped around Scruggs' picking fingers helped produce the hard, twangy sound, Stover fashioned a set from a discarded Prince Albert tobacco can.

Later in 1945 Monroe had hired a singer and guitar player named Lester Flatt. Born in 1914 in Overton County, Tennessee, Flatt first learned to play the banjo from his father. When the clawhammer technique proved elusive, he switched to guitar and by the time he was in his twenties, he played semi-professionally with several bands while working in a textile mill. The Blue Grass Boys was not Flatt's first job with a Monroe, for he had sung tenor with Charlie Monroe's group in 1943. But Flatt's pleasant, slightly nasal voice was better suited for singing lead parts, which was his role in the Blue Grass Boys. Pickers became well acquainted with Flatt's guitar work, especially his "G-run." Based on an open G chord, the run has become a classic way to begin a tune and end verses and choruses.*

Being a member of the Blue Grass Boys was no picnic. Endless weeks of touring and sleeping in a car took its toll as they worked all over the eastern half of the country, racing

---

* Starting on a G note (on the low E string), it moves to the open A string, a slide on that string from B♭ to B, then the open D string, a hammer-on on the E note, back to the open D string, and ending on the open G string.

back each week to Nashville for a Saturday night appearance on *Grand Ole Opry*. Scruggs was about ready to return to North Carolina and forget about professional music when Flatt announced that he too was about to give notice. The two men decided to form their own band, one with a less frenetic schedule than Monroe's. They called themselves the Foggy Mountain Boys, after the Carter Family's song "Foggy Mountain Top." Initial personnel consisted of Scruggs, Flatt, Jimmy Shumate on fiddle, and Cedric Rainwater on bass. Later that year Mac Wiseman joined to sing tenor to Flatt's lead, but he left in 1949 to work with the Blue Grass Boys. Wiseman's place was taken by Curly Seckler, whose instrument was the mandolin. The band played on the *Farm and Fun Hour* show over Bristol, Virginia's WCYB, and later moved its base of operations to Knoxville.

If Flatt and Scruggs were trying to find a respite from traveling, their popularity did not permit much time at home. They signed with Mercury Records and spent the next few years playing on radio and making personal appearances in the Knoxville area. Conditions were not always the best. Flatt remembers one engagement in Virginia that was held in someone's barn. A rainstorm started, the owner's cattle sought shelter, and suddenly the pickin' and singin' of the Foggy Mountain Boys included a chorus of bovine bawling. Eventually, the band's reputation reached a representative of the Martha White Flour Company, who approached them about appearing on their own radio program. Flatt and Scruggs accepted and moved to Nashville in 1953. Thereafter thousands of people woke up at 5:45 a.m. five days a week to the band's playing the Martha White theme. In addition to weekday shows, there were Saturday evening and Sunday morning programs. Once they were able to tape shows the Foggy Mountain Boys began a circuit of live and recorded performances that added up to a weekly total of 2,500 miles.

Scruggs wrote "Foggy Mountain Breakdown" in 1948, and

Roger Sprung

The Foggy Mountain Boys performing on WNOX, Knoxville, during the 1950s, Earl Scruggs on banjo and Lester Flatt on guitar

it immediately became a banjo picker's showpiece. Other much-requested numbers were "Salty Dog," "Doin' My Time," "Cabin in Caroline," and a version of the Carter Family's "Jimmy Brown the Newsboy" with Scruggs playing lead guitar. However, his primary interest was still the banjo. Ever since childhood Scruggs had been intrigued with the idea of being able to change keys in the middle of a tune. Toward that end, he devised "tuners," two cams attached to the banjo's second and third strings and mounted between the tuning pegs. Twisting them permitted a rapid and accurate modulation from the key of G to D (the cams lowered the G string to F♯ and the B string to A). Two of Scruggs' original compositions, "Flint Hill Special" and "Earl's Breakdown," displayed the tuners to best advantage.

An automobile accident in 1955 kept Scruggs off stage for approximately a year and a half. Although Donny Bryant was able to substitute on five-string, the Foggy Mountain Boys found another lead instrument in Buck Graves' Dobro. The unamplified steel guitar had not been associated with Bluegrass until Graves joined the band. His left hand fretting the instrument with a steel bar, "Uncle Josh" (as his nickname suggests, Graves did comedy bits with the band) turned the Dobro into a powerful lead voice, slipping and swooping like a barnstorming biplane. He remained with the Boys and inspired many young musicians: Jerry Douglas, who plays Dobro with the Country Gentlemen, raced home after hearing Graves to raise his guitar's bridge and experiment fretting with a piece of metal pipe.*

By the time they appeared at the first Newport Folk Festival in 1958, the Foggy Mountain Boys were charter members of the folk revival. There was an immediate response to the banjo, which set urban toes tapping as hard as their rural counterparts. College and concert dates west of the Mississippi and north of the Mason-Dixon Line quickly followed, and Earl's disciples multiplied. Pawn shops and antique stores did a land-office business in used banjos, while music shops were deluged with orders for Foggy Mountain Boys albums (the band changed label to Columbia in 1960). If there was no one in the neighborhood to teach the technique, the only way to catch all of Scruggs' galaxy of notes was to play records at slow speed. Although it was a slow and frustrating process, this way of solving the mysteries of the "5–3–1–5" roll made the hours (or days) spent hunched over the phonograph and banjo seem worthwhile. Meanwhile, fledgling Flatt turned their vocal and guitar attentions from "Rock around the Clock" and "Diana" to "Blue Ridge Mountain Home" and "Little Maggie." Before long, campus quads and city parks were alive with the sound of Bluegrass.

As if in response to the folk revival, the sound of the Foggy

---

* Substantially in response to Graves' popularizing the instrument, the Dobro Company, which had stopped manufacturing these guitars, resumed production in 1956.

Mountain Boys changed during the early 1960s. Several albums made during that period displayed less "hard-driving" picking and mountain harmonies. They included songs from other branches of folk music, such as the campfire standard "Down in the Valley" and Woody Guthrie's "This Land Is Your Land." But record producers who might have thought that urban audiences cared only for this kind of Bluegrass weren't entirely correct. At the band's 1961 concert at Carnegie Hall, one of the most persistently requested numbers was, to Flatt's delighted surprise, "The Martha White Theme."

Two other themes increased Flatt's and Scruggs' nationwide success. When television producer Paul Henning heard the band during a California appearance, he hired them to play the theme song of *The Beverly Hillbillies*. Moviegoers heard Scruggs' picking when in 1967 "Foggy Mountain Breakdown" became better known as the theme from *Bonnie and Clyde*. Both tunes reached the Hit Parade, whereupon the Foggy Mountain Boys were besieged with requests to appear on television programs outside the South.

As they performed around the country, exposure to other kinds of music caused Scruggs to reassess where his banjo playing was (and was not) heading. While in Chicago to tape a 1960 television special, he joined a jam session with King Curtis, the rhythm-and-blues saxaphonist.* Scruggs began to discover that the five-string had a potential for music other than Bluegrass. He listened to some more contemporary music, not terribly difficult in a family with teenage boys. As his sons Randy and Gary learned to play electric guitar and bass, their father accompanied their rock music, as natural to him as leading them through "Black Mountain Rag" or "Sally Goodwin."

Another artist recording on Columbia was Bob Dylan. The

* Rock 'n' roll fans will remember Curtis' work on several of the Coasters' hits, especially "Yakkity-Yak."

Foggy Mountain Boys' producer suggested that they include some of Dylan's songs on their albums, and although sales increased, Lester Flatt was not happy. He felt that contemporary songs were wrong for his voice and style. Matters reached a breaking point, and Flatt and Scruggs went their separate ways in 1969.

Scruggs' route led to increased involvement in "modern" music. He formed the Earl Scruggs Revue, with Randy and Gary on guitar and bass. For a while Vassar Clements (a Blue Grass Boy alumnus) played fiddle with them, knocking audiences over with a supersonic version of "Orange Blossom Special." Another "old-timer" was Uncle "Josh" (Buck) Graves, who after a stint with Lester Flatt's band, felt that he too had reached a limit with traditional Bluegrass. The Revue plays Dylan, Joni Mitchell, and the Beatles, as well as "Salty Dog" and "Foggy Mountain Breakdown": although Scruggs' picking hasn't changed over twenty-five years on the latter, the Bluegrass standards are now done to thunderously amplified accompaniment. And when the Revue launches into "Reuben," some in the audience may wonder whether Scruggs ever thinks of the day when his three-finger style sprang out of that tune.

After their parting of the ways, Flatt returned to more traditional Bluegrass. He formed the Nashville Grass, a band that has included former Foggy Mountain Boys Paul Warren, "Uncle Jake" Tullock, and Uncle Josh Graves. Flatt continued with the Martha White sponsorship and its 5:45 a.m. WSM radio program ("live" on tape).

Some Bluegrass fans have short memories. When Scruggs' name is mentioned, they reply, "Phooey, he doesn't play Bluegrass anymore." Earl would be the first to agree. What he's doing now is, well, just music. But as ready as purists are to dismiss Scruggs for what he's now doing, they would do well to give a thought to how many banjo pickers, both rural and urban, he has inspired. Maybe he was just in the right place at the right time, but indisputably he was there. He was there with Bill Monroe on *Grand Ole Opry* for so many people to hear his style, and both he and Lester Flatt were there to entertain audiences around the country and to introduce them to Bluegrass. And he was there to help link traditional and contemporary music and musicians, attracting people from disparate backgrounds; to discover all kinds of rural music.*

Several years ago, a long-haired picker sat on a New York City park bench, concentrating on his banjo as though a booking on *Grand Ole Opry* depended on it. His toe tapped against his banjo case on which "H F E" was stenciled in psychedelic colors. When a passerby asked what the letters stood for, his grin stretched a country mile: "Hooray For Earl!"

---

* Two albums show how Scruggs has spanned this generational Cumberland Gap. "Earl Scruggs: His Family and Friends," based on an NET documentary, features down-home pickin' with the Morris Brothers and Doc Watson on one hand, and Dylan, Joan Baez, and the Byrds on the other. Along with such traditionalists as Jimmy Martin and Mother Maybelle Carter, he appears on "Will the Circle Be Unbroken" backed by the founders of the recorded feast, country-rockers the Nitty Gritty Dirt Band.

SIX THE SPREAD OF BLUEGRASS

As soon as rural musicians discovered that Monroe and Flatt and Scruggs were mining gold from hill-country music, string bands underwent a renaissance. Banjos came down from attics, grandfathers were asked to demonstrate shuffle bowing on fiddles, and guitar picks cracked as players worked on G-runs. The result was that almost every southern town had at least one band eager to be paid for playing "just like the Blue Grass Boys." *

Even guessing at the number of professional Bluegrass groups over the past twenty-five years is an impossibility. Some were formed only for a specific recording session or one-night stand. Others might have tried to remain together, but were forced by economic necessity to disband. Some have spread reputations no further than their own neighborhoods, while still others have ended as their leaders retired or died. Nevertheless there were—and are—many.

The bands discussed in this chapter are the best-known of the current practitioners, the stars of festivals and concerts. Each represents a different aspect of Bluegrass. Ralph and Carter Stanley are identified with traditional mountain music. The Lewis Family is a gospel group. Jimmy Martin demonstrates how an entertainer's personality can contribute to his success. Don Reno has a distinctive banjo style and affection for jazz material. Jim and Jesse McReynolds have drifted toward other kinds of country music, while maintaining ties with older mountain music. The Osborne

* It was not until the late 1950s that this kind of music became known as Bluegrass. Before that time, and even to some of its practitioners now, it's called "country music" or "mountain music."

Brothers are sometimes labeled Bluegrass-rock, while the Country Gentlemen are exponents of "progressive" Bluegrass.

These last two bands cause definitional problems for some purists, who feel that unless the music is done in a "traditional" manner (that is, à la Monroe-Flatt-&-Scruggs-Martin-Stanley Brothers), the result just isn't Bluegrass. Others point out that like other forms of country music, Bluegrass has never been static. A Beatles song or a set of drums should therefore be considered as likely or as acceptable as a ragtime tune or Dobro guitar was years ago. For those who feel a need to distinguish between traditional and progressive or rock Bluegrass, here's a rule of thumb: a traditional band won't play modern stuff, but a progressive band will play both modern and traditional. In less abstract terms, you can't be sure whether a band is traditional or progressive if it starts with "Salty Dog," "Blue Moon of Kentucky," and then "Knoxville Girl." But as soon as the group launches into a Mozart concerto, Broadway hit, or top-ten tune, you can be sure you're hearing progressive Bluegrass.

No matter what the category, bands continue to draw from time-honored lyric themes for their repertoire. First and foremost is love, sometimes fulfilled but more often unrequited or unsuccessful. Longing for the familiar is another overriding theme: a yen to return home, whether literally to one's birthplace or metaphorically to share a spiritual afterlife with one's kith and kin.

Musicians also share certain characteristics. Growing up in areas which were the source of mountain music, the men were taught to pick and sing by friends and neighbors. Some first gained reputations over local radio shows, then moved to larger stations, and finally found national prominence. Timing played a crucial part in success: being at the right time at the right place led to joining "name" bands and obtaining radio and record contracts when they decided to go out on their own. The roots and branches of family trees, as the text indicates, quickly became a Spanish-moss entanglement of genealogy. None of these people has become wealthy from string-band music, yet all express a strong feeling of satisfaction over being able to entertain with and perpetuate the kind of music they care so much about.

THE STANLEY BROTHERS

Carter Stanley was born in 1925, Ralph two years later in the Clinch Mountain community of Nora, Virginia. Both brothers learned to play instruments at early ages. Carter's first guitar came through a mail-order catalogue and, appropriately enough, a local postman taught him the basic chords. Ralph learned the banjo from his mother, who in fact taught the instrument to all her children—music was one of the few recreational activities on the Stanley's isolated farm. When Carter left military service after World War II, he and Ralph formed the Clinch Mountain Boys. Their first professional appearance was in Norton, Virginia, their second over nearby Bristol's WCYB *Farm and Fun Hour*. Although Ralph contends that the band never imitated any other group, their 1948 recording of "Molly and Tenbrooks" has often been cited as the first unmistakable influence of Monroe's Blue Grass Boys on other string bands. However, the Stanley Brothers had their own distinctive sound. Ralph's voice had a timbre frequently described as "high and lonesome," which when coupled with Carter's, sent shivers of delight down audiences' spines. Another element was the instrumentals, somewhere between Monroe's more polished sound and the roughhewn string bands of the twenties and thirties.

Except for a short time when Carter played with the Blue Grass Boys because Ralph was recuperating from an accident, the brothers played together until Carter's death in

Ralph Stanley

1966. They were among the first to appear at college concerts outside the South and tour in Europe and the Orient.

Ralph Stanley continued the Clinch Mountain Boys after Carter's death and the band became something of a memorial to the dead brother. Two young men who joined the group in 1969, Keith Whitley and Ricky Skaggs, had impressed Ralph with their uncanny resemblance to his and Carter's voices.* He was so smitten with their adherence to the "old music" that it was understood that Whitley and Skaggs would inherit the band when he retired. But as Skaggs points out, "That won't be for years. The longer Ralph works the better he gets."

Ralph Stanley's music has deep roots in the past. The Clinch Mountain Boys' repertoire, with its *a capella* gospel quartets, occasional clawhammer banjo solos, and fiddle and banjo duets, link Bluegrass with older Appalachian ballads and breakdowns.

THE LEWIS FAMILY

A trip through the Shenandoah Valley, the Blue Ridge Mountains, and other parts of the southern Appalachians gives an insight into many of the influences on the area's residents. The changing hues of maple and birch leaves in autumn are breathtaking but brief. Winter's bleakness reflects the dour struggle against nature which has so long been a part of mountain folks' heritage. But as evergreen trees stand as verdant symbols above fallen snow, there is always a promise of spring and of nature's literal and spiritual resurrection. Small wonder that hill-country people possess a deep religious faith.

Country music has always reflected a basic belief in the Bible's teachings, and Bluegrass is no exception. No perfor-

* See page 79 for more on Skaggs.

The Lewis Family

mance, even by a "new-grass" band, is without at least one gospel number, and few festivals fail to include a gospel-Bluegrass act.

The Lewis Family is one such group. They are indeed a family act: sisters Miggie, Janis and Polly,* brothers Wallace, Talmadge and "Little Roy," and father "Pop" ("Mom" Lewis works behind the scenes, creating the girls' wardrobes and selling records at concerts). The family grew up in a deeply religious environment where secular songs, especially if sung by women, would have been far too worldy. Influenced by the Monroe and Louvin Brothers, the Blue Grass Boys, and Flatt and Scruggs, the Lewises took up mountain instruments to spread God's word through music. The family began its professional career in 1951, and since 1954 has been performing regularly over WJBF-TV in Atlanta. The Lewises moved out of the deep South to mountain-music areas, and eventually joined the Bluegrass festival and concert circuit.

A Lewis Family performance is in the spirit of down-home camp meetings and revival tent shows. Their music provides the sermonizing, and just a brief and random sample of titles reflects their songs' message: "I Do Believe," "We Shall Gather at the River," "Honey in the Rock," and "You Go to Your Church (and I'll Go to Mine)." Their shows, however, are far from staid and predictable. Wearing bouffant hairdos

---

* The participation of the Lewis sisters is an exception that proves a rule. Bluegrass is almost an exclusively male province, most likely because the early bands—the Blue Grass Boys, the Foggy Mountain Boys, the Stanley Brothers, etc.—had no women members, and people just assumed that Bluegrass (like its string-band precursor) was a fraternity. There is also an older reason: like their colleagues in the acting profession, musicians have been associated with loose living, so playing in a band was considered too damaging to a woman's reputation.

Reputations were secure, however, by performing in the company of relatives, for what could be more family entertainment than entertainment by a family (as in Sara, A.P., and Maybelle Carter)? Hymns and gospel songs were always acceptable fare for women both in and out of church, so that the Lewis girls should "spread God's message" publicly through song is thoroughly in keeping with fundamentalist morality. And on an amateur basis, women continued to sing and play as homespun entertainment; most Bluegrassmen learned ballads and tunes from mothers, grandmothers, and other female relatives.

The Lewis Family a few years later

and matching dresses, the girls harmonize to the rhythm of
their tambourines and to the guitar, fiddle, mandolin, bass,
and five-string played by Wallace, Talmadge, Pop, and Little
Roy.

A connecting link between gospel and Bluegrass is found
in Little Roy Lewis, acknowledged as one of the best banjo
pickers in the business. His ebullient stage presence blends
well with his solo and backup instrumental work to capture
the attention of even the most impious members of an audience. One particular anecdote reveals his group's place in
Bluegrass. The Lewis Family appeared several years ago at
an outdoor concert at Vanderbilt University on the same bill
as the Blue Grass Boys. After the family had finished their
segment, and the most blasé collegians had stopped clapping
and stomping to their music, Bill Monroe invited Little Roy
to join his band for a number. Lewis demurred. "Mr.
Monroe, you'll have to ask my parents' permission." Pop

Lewis gave his assent, but "Just as long as you-all don't play any profane songs." After a short off-microphone conference, Monroe and the elder Lewis settled on "Cripple Creek," whereupon Little Roy joined the Blue Grass Boys for five minutes of some of the best picking to echo through downtown Nashville in many years.

JIMMY MARTIN

Jimmy Martin was born in 1927 in Sneedville, Tennessee. At the age of thirteen he bought his first guitar and would walk five miles to a neighbor's house for lessons. The Blue Grass Boys were among Martin's favorite performers, and in 1949 he went to Nashville to see them on *Grand Ole Opry*. Actually, Martin had an ulterior motive. Going backstage, he introduced himself to Bill Monroe, saying that he too was a singer. Monroe gave him an audition and hired him on the spot.

After four years of singing lead and playing guitar with the Blue Grass Boys, Martin left to organize a group of his own. Named the Sunny Mountain Boys, the band at one time included Bobby and Sonny Osborne. Martin and the band were regulars on Wheeling, West Virginia's *WWVA Jamboree* and on radio and television programs in Michigan, and Louisiana.

Martin adheres to his own kind of tradition. He insists that his band, regardless of personnel, remain faithful to the "Martin sound"; he feels that "audiences come out to hear tunes the way they heard them on my records." His repertoire is known for its "novelty" numbers, unselfconscious lyrics of the "she's leaving me but she'll be sorry" variety.

The word for Jimmy Martin is "entertainer." He will joke and cajole with audiences, occasionally launching into ten-minute monologues about whatever strikes his fancy. But

Steve Arkin

Jimmy Martin on guitar with the Sunny Mountain Boys

when it's time to play, Martin calls on the Sunny Mountain Boys for their hard-driving sound, the perfect (and almost the only possible) setting for Martin's ebullient, dynamic performances.

DON RENO

The two dominant styles of Bluegrass banjo are the "Scruggs-style" rolls and the chromatic single-notes as developed by Bobby Thompson and Bill Keith. A third style known as "plectrum" is characteristic of Don Reno, one of the least imitated yet most admired of Bluegrass musicians.

Reno was born in 1927 in Spartanburg, South Carolina. He started playing the banjo at the age of five, and the guitar a year later. Familiar with Snuffy Jenkins' three-finger banjo style through radio and records, Reno went as a nine-year-old hopeful to see him perform. Jenkins took him aside backstage and explained the technique: "Put another pick on that third finger and use it if it kills you."

Playing with the Morris Brothers was Reno's first professional job in music. He had been with an amateur band when
Zeke Morris, impressed by his playing, invited Reno to join
his own group. (Reno is among the many country musicians
who feels that the Morris Brothers had the first Bluegrass
band, with the purely traditional instrumentation and vocal
style.)

Reno's path crossed that of Earl Scruggs, whom he succeeded as a member of the Morris Brothers. Then, when in
1943, Bill Monroe wanted to hire Reno, Reno said his plans
were subject to being accepted for military service. Reno
went into the army, and on his discharge was surprised to
hear people say that he played like Scruggs. "That was something of a turnaround," he says, "because Earl was playing
the way I did before I went into the service." *

Returning to South Carolina after the war, Reno ran a gro-
cery store and played banjo only on weekends. One evening
in 1948 he was listening to the Blue Grass Boys on *Grand
Ole Opry*. He didn't hear Scruggs with the band and thought
to himself, "I'll take the job." Reno drove to Nashville, only
to learn that the group had left for a North Carolina engagement, and he took off in hot pursuit. By the time he found
where they were performing, the band was already on stage.
Reno took his banjo out of its case, walked out next to
Monroe, and started to play. One minor inconvenience was
that he had forgotten his capo; he recalls that "it seemed they
were playing in sharps and flats all night."

Reno stayed with the Blue Grass Boys until May of the
next year. During that time he refined a technique of playing
melodies by picking two notes simultaneously, duplicating
the double-note style of fiddle and guitar playing. Reno
found it particularly useful on slow songs where rolls did not

* The two men remain good friends. In fact, Reno plays a banjo once owned by
Scruggs, for which he swapped one that had belonged to Snuffy Jenkins.

Roger Sprung

Don Reno (*left*) **and Red Smiley in 1950**

N. Ville

Don Reno, Buck Ryan, Bill Harrell, and Ed Ferris
(*left to right*) **in New York City, 1974**

fit the tempo (he now uses it at all speeds, interspersing it with three-finger rolls).*

Moving to Roanoke, Reno met another Blue Grass Boys alumnus, Tommy Magness, who had come from Nashville with a singer-guitarist named Red Smiley. They formed a band which was first called the Tennessee Buddies, then the Tennessee Cut-Ups. Making a living from music was difficult in those days; as Reno says, he knew the best kind of pasteboard to line shoes with and the cheapest places to eat. The Cut-Ups broke up in 1952, and Reno rejoined Arthur Smith, a tenor-banjo player with whom he had formerly worked. One of their compositions was "Mocking Banjos," the "Dueling Banjos" of the film *Deliverance*. Later that year Reno and Smiley revived the Tennessee Cut-Ups, and played at concerts, clubs, and festivals; two highlights in their career have

---

* Although Reno calls his style chromatic, "plectrum" (the manner of playing tenor banjo) is more accurate, especially since "chromatic" is used to describe the manner in which Thompson and Keith play.

been performances at the United Nations and at the 1968 presidential inauguration. (After Smiley's death in 1972, Bill Harrell took over on guitar and lead vocals).

In an effort to widen his audience, Reno includes popular songs of the twenties and thirties. He feels that people who recognize tunes such as "Twelfth Street Rag" or "The Washington and Lee Swing" may find them more enjoyable when played in Bluegrass style. The Cut-Ups also play traditional string-band music, but the band's performance has none of the on-stage reticence typical of some other Bluegrass groups. Reflecting Reno's early days in music when a string band did comedy routines, it's a time for ebullient good-time picking and singing.

JIM AND JESSE McREYNOLDS

Another pair of brothers from the Clinch Mountains, Jim and Jesse McReynolds were born in Coeburn, Virginia: Jim in 1927 and Jesse two years later. Mountain music came naturally to the boys; their grandfather was a champion fiddler in the region, and they were particularly attracted to the fraternal duet style of the 1930s. Jim took up the guitar, Jesse learned the mandolin, and together they harmonized in the fluid manner of the Delmore, Louvin, and Bolick Brothers.

Like Ralph and Carter Stanley, the McReynolds made their radio debut on WNVA in Norton, Virginia, in 1947. They played unaffected mountain-style string-band music until 1951, at which time the brothers and their band experimented with other elements of country music, such as a pedal steel guitar and drums. The group's name was changed in 1952 to Jim and Jesse and the Virginia Boys. Several years after Jesse finished his military obligation, the band moved to the Starday label. One of their records, "Border Ride," subsequently became something of a landmark in Bluegrass as the first recorded example of chromatic banjo picking.

Clark Thomas

Jesse (*left*) and Jim McReynolds

The McReynolds became regulars on *Grand Ole Opry* in 1964. The success of other performers who had adopted more contemporary country sounds encouraged them to move away from straight Bluegrass. An album of that period consisted of Chuck Berry rock 'n' roll songs. Another, "Diesel on My Tail," had songs celebrating truck drivers and a strong electrified sound. The album and its title song became nationwide hits.

Despite their excursions into modern country music, Jim and Jesse never strayed very far from their Clinch Mountains heritage. Their band returned to traditional instrumentation, which included the work of a procession of excellent banjo pickers. These included Bobby Thompson, a pioneer in the chromatic style (as on "Border Ride"); Allen Shelton, whose playing is marked by an emphatic "bounce"; Carl Jackson, who went on to the Glen Campbell television show; and Vic Jordan.

A distinctive feature of the band is Jesse's mandolin playing. In addition to playing melodies with tremolos and slides, he devised a technique known as "crosspicking," analogous to three-finger-style banjo rolls. The highest set of strings sounds as a drone, while tunes are produced by the second and third sets fretted along the instrument's neck up to the octave. The right hand picks a steady arpeggio of triplets: a downstroke on the third set of strings followed by upstrokes on the first and second sets. On some solos, Jesse frets only one of a pair of strings to make it sound in harmony with the other.

BOBBY AND SONNY OSBORNE

Bobby Osborne was born in 1931 in Hyden, Kentucky. His first instrument was the guitar, and after several years of playing modern country music, he discovered Bluegrass through banjo player Larry Richardson. He, Richardson, and the Cline brothers played together as the Lonesome Pine Fiddlers, a band with a strong mountain-music sound.

Six years younger than his brother, Sonny Osborne learned to play the banjo while Bobby served in the Korean War. At the age of thirteen he was playing with the Lonesome Pine Fiddlers when Jimmy Martin introduced him to Bill Monroe, who gave him a position in the Blue Grass Boys. Sonny's first appearance with the band was on *Grand Ole Opry*, and Monroe did little to dispel the youngster's nervousness: instead of speaking directly to Sonny, he passed messages through Martin.

When Bobby left the army, the brothers decided to form their own act. But first they joined Martin and the Sunny

MCA Records

The Osborne Brothers

Mountain Boys in 1953 (because both he and Martin played guitars, Bobby switched to mandolin). They then left two years later to go out on their own. Their new band experimented within the perimeters of traditional Bluegrass with more flexible harmonies, using two banjos on some numbers, and including an electric bass.

Performing with non-Bluegrass country acts, the Osbornes felt that their string-band instrumentation sounded weak in comparison. They decided to go "modern" in 1967, attaching amplification equipment to their banjo and mandolin and adding electric guitars, piano, and a set of drums to the group. The Osbornes' repertoire extended into other kinds of country music, even going to the extent of including a string section in one number.

Another step was Sonny's adding a sixth string to his banjo. Placed between the fourth and fifth strings, it is tuned to a G one octave below the third string.

When the "modern" Osborne Brothers first appeared at Bluegrass festivals, reaction was vehement (one irate fan went so far as to cut the cord to the banjo's amplifier). But for everyone who winced at what the Osbornes were doing, many more tapped their toes and bought records. Some Bluegrass musicians were inspired to go beyond acoustic instrumentation. The lesson of Bobby and Sonny Osborne has been that Bluegrass, and the "Nashville sound" are not necessarily exclusive.

THE COUNTRY GENTLEMEN

In addition to being the seat of sundry government activities, Washington, D.C. is also the nation's unofficial Bluegrass capital. Beginning in the 1930s, people moved away from the hill country when they could not find employment at home, and to thousands from Virginia, North Carolina, and eastern Kentucky, one of the nearest large cities was Washington. It was a good place for professional and part-time pickers; audiences that had grown up on string-band music filled clubs from Baltimore to northern Virginia.

It was in Washington that the Country Gentlemen came into existence, appropriately enough on the Fourth of July. The year was 1957, and a singer-guitar player named Charlie Waller was asked by a friend to fill in at a night-club appear-

The Country Gentlemen (*left to right*: Rick Skaggs, Jerry Douglas, Doyle Lawson, James Bailey, Bill Yates, Charlie Waller)

ance. Waller's friend had also brought along John Duffy, a mandolin player. The result of this one-night stand was a decision to form a band which Waller and Duffy dubbed the Country Gentlemen.

Charlie Waller was born in 1935 in Jointerville, Texas. Raised in Louisiana's cotton country, he learned to play the guitar at the age of ten. Waller moved to the Washington area as a teenager, then went back to Louisiana to work on country-music radio and television shows, returning to Washington for good in 1957. By contrast, Duffy, who was born in 1934, grew up in the capital district. He learned the mandolin when he was nineteen, and although proficient on the instrument, Duffy treated music as an avocation until he met Waller.

The Gents acquired their distinctive sound when Eddie Adcock joined the group in 1959. Born in 1938 in Scottsville, Virginia, Adcock was well versed in traditional Bluegrass, having first played banjo with Mac Wiseman, and later with Bill Monroe and the Blue Grass Boys.

Several elements set the Country Gentlemen apart from other bands performing in those days. There were Waller's distinctive "throaty" lead voice and the group's smooth trio and quartet harmonies. Duffy, who also played Dobro, often plucked two or three sets of strings simultaneously during mandolin breaks to produce a jazzy effect. Adcock's banjo style showed the influence of guitar finger-picking, particularly the syncopated patterns of Merle Travis. In addition, the band experimented with tunes from outside the usual string-band repertoire, such as the British ballad "Greensleeves" and the theme from the motion picture *Exodus.*

In 1961 the Country Gentlemen appeared at Carnegie Hall in New York and at Oberlin College, the first year of many dates in the North. Urban audiences found their brand of music more "palatable" than the kind played by other Bluegrass groups. The Gents remained associated with the Washington area, appearing regularly at the Shamrock night club (later the Cellar Door) in Georgetown. Like other Bluegrass bands, they joined the summer-festival circuit and recorded for "specialty" labels.

Waller remains the only member of the original band. Bill Emerson, who had played banjo with the Gents during their early days, returned to replace Adcock, then left in 1974 to head the U.S. Navy's Bluegrass band, Country Current. John Duffy became tired with the rigors of travel and left in 1969 (he now plays with the Seldom Scene). The group recently moved to a fuller sound by adding fiddle and Dobro players.

A Country Gentlemen performance displays the wide variety found in progressive Bluegrass. There are such nuggets from the traditional lode as "Sally Goodwin" and "Train 45," as well as *a capella* gospel quartets. But from there the repertoire moves out of the public domain into the realm of pop songs: John Prine's "Paradise," which describes the effect of strip mining in Kentucky, the Beatles' "Yesterday," and Kris Kristofferson's "Casey's Last Ride" with imagery that reflects a close reading of T. S. Eliot. The total effect is enough to blur any Mason-Dixon Line between rural and urban music. And lest one think that the Gents' appeal is limited only to "progressives," a *Muleskinner News* poll resulted in the group's election as "Band of the Year" for 1971, 1972, and 1973.

SEVEN ᴛ HREE PICKERS

The previous chapter dealt with the major bands and focused on their leaders. Now, however, let's focus on three men whose biographies offer different views of Bluegrass. Vic Jordan has been a member of four of those major bands and provides a behind-the-scenes glimpse of a journeyman musician's life. Ricky Skaggs' connection with both traditional and contemporary string bands reveals a profound involvement in the music, and his career is one answer to the question of where the next generation of pickers is coming from. And since urbanites' interest and success in rural music is an important element, Roger Sprung typifies that facet of old-timey and Bluegrass music.

VIC JORDAN

Born in 1939 in Washington, D.C., Vic Jordan discovered Bluegrass at the age of seventeen, thanks to a band called the Cripple Creek Boys:

They were playing in Norfolk, Virginia on WCMS. I went down there and tried to watch and pick up some licks. I was just learning at that time . . . I hardly knew how to tune the banjo, much less play it. The banjo was the first instrument I ever tried to study. What really got me excited and interested to do something with the banjo was Jim Eanes's Shenandoah Valley Boys when Allen Shelton was playing banjo. Allen really impressed me; he could make you sit there and bounce both feet off the floor in time with him. He had that little drivy bounce that makes you want to climb the walls.

I practiced every chance I could get. At that time you couldn't get people to show you things, so I slowed down records to catch the notes, just pure imitation. I recommend that to beginning banjo players: work a lot from the records. Study the clichés, and eventually you'll hear things on your own and have the ability to create on your own. The first records I was able to get my hands on was Don Reno stuff. Next I got Earl Scruggs' "Foggy Mountain Special" and "Foggy Mountain Breakdown."

Jordan's first professional band was a local group in Lake Charles, Louisiana, when he was in the Air Force:

We'd make five or ten bucks apiece sometimes, but it wasn't really professional. You know, they say you're professional if you make money at it, but I don't believe that. I think you're professional if you make a living at it. That's the difference: if that's your livelihood, then you're a professional.

We played at outhouse openings, anything—you name it, we played there. I was still doing Reno stuff for my instrumentals, with what I thought were his flourishes. I can look back and see they weren't. I just thought they were. When you get to talking about guys like Reno, Scruggs, and Bobby Thompson, you think you've learned a certain passage. Then you go back and every time you listen to it, you find out something you missed.

Jordan worked with Jimmy Martin briefly in 1964, leaving to join Wilma Lee and Stoney Cooper, an act that mixed Bluegrass with pure country music. In 1966 he went back to Martin:

The hard drive that Jimmy demands wasn't as difficult as getting the licks exactly like J.D. [J. D. Crowe, Jordan's predecessor with the Sunny Mountain Boys], getting the turns and breaks exact. Jimmy wanted them just like the record. He wants his music to be "his sound." Anytime you hear his music you'll hear it the same way. He wants that continuity of sound. For a long time I felt that I could absorb what he had to teach—and he can teach you a lot.

Jordan stayed with Martin for eleven months:

I had a discussion with Jimmy, we were both open about it. I told him that I knew I wasn't playing to suit him and that I didn't feel it was what I wanted to play. It would be best, I said, if he looked for

Steve Arkin

Vic Jordan on banjo with Jim and Jesse

another banjo player and I looked for something else. So I hung up the phone.

It wasn't thirty minutes before Jim Monroe called and said that Lamar Grier had left and that his daddy wanted to know whether I still wanted the job (I had talked with Bill Monroe a few times and told him I'd like to play with him sometime).

And so Vic became a member of the Blue Grass Boys. It was a time of serious study for him:

I think I learned a lot of things that really mattered: what to look for in the tone of an instrument. Bill Monroe had a lot of influence on my timing. He taught me there's a difference between speed and quickness. Quickness has to do with the individual note, while speed is one note after the other. Quickness is touch; like Monroe said once, "Everyone thinks I'm fast, but I'm not, I'm quick."

He's a stickler for melody, too. When it's instrumental time, he wants to hear tone, time, and melody. No razzmatazz. Now when he's singing, Monroe wants good solid drive and good fill behind him, good pretty stuff, but don't get flaky back there. When it's your turn to play, then let 'em have it.

It was a matter of money that made Jordan switch to Lester Flatt and the Nashville Grass in 1968.

It was straight salary versus play by the day with Monroe. Of course I liked Flatt's music. I always admired Flatt and Scruggs, so it was a chance to get paid well and join up with some tradition too. And talk about nervous! I was coming in behind what most people consider "The Man" in banjo playing. Finally, after a few days I just had a talk with myself and said, "Look, all I can do is the best I'm able, and if that's not good enough, well, so be it."

Lester never told me what to play. When I went to work for him, I asked him, "Do you want me to imitate Earl? I don't think I can do that. I may imitate some of his licks, but nobody can imitate Earl." And he said, "You play 'em like you feel 'em."

Things don't worry Flatt much. It's sort of like he's thinking: "I'm going out there relaxed. If they like me, OK, and if not, well, there's another town tomorrow." If he feels pressure, he doesn't show it. You've got to admire him for it.

But working with the "big-band" sound of the Nashville Grass had certain creative limitations for Vic:

The most disappointing thing about the group was that there were so many lead instruments—seven pieces, so all the breaks worked out to be split breaks for everybody. You would just be getting started in a break and you'd have to quit, and then you had to be quiet because someone else was doing backup. It was divided up so much that you kinda came off the stage frustrated, feeling like you never had a chance to play.

Then too, Lester wanted to try two banjos. I felt I wasn't doing enough as one. Not that I had anything against Haskell McCormick [the band's other banjo player]. I've known him for years, but they asked me what I thought and I said I didn't think much of it. We did some stuff on the road, and it was well received, I think, because of our choice of material. We did "Old Joe Clark," "Foggy Mountain Breakdown," and several others. Haskell did the lead and I worked out the harmony. The difficult part of the harmony is getting both three-finger rolls so that they work out exactly together, so it sounds really professional.

Jordan left the Nashville Grass after two years with them. Having grown a little tired of traveling, he took a job at home in Nashville, handling dynamite in a quarry (a skill he had learned in the Air Force). Then it was back to Bluegrass with

Jim and Jesse. Playing banjo with the Virginia Boys, Vic was in the spot formerly held by two of his idols, Allen Shelton and Bobby Thompson. Thompson is a particular favorite:

As far as naming the best all-around banjo player in the country, I think he's it. I've heard him do tenor stuff, I've heard him play single notes like Reno, the straight Scruggs drive, the Shelton bounce, his own chromatics, and anything else you can think of, and I think Bobby is the finest there is. I played bass with Jim and Jesse (which was a disaster because I'm no bass player, but I wanted to get with the group so bad that I'd have done anything). Anyway, I watched Bobby play and do some fantastic things. But the people just looked at each other like "When are we going to hear some breakdowns?" And now Bobby's doing nothing but recording studio work and everybody says, "I wish we could see Bobby Thompson."

In March of 1974 Jordan informed Jim and Jesse that he wanted to leave the band, like Thompson, to work at studio recording sessions. Another event in his career took place that month: at the inauguration of Grand Ole Opry's new auditorium, which included a visit by President Nixon, it was Vic Jordan who picked "Hail to the Chief" on the five-string.

RICKY SKAGGS

Ricky Skaggs was born in 1954 in Cordell, a small town in eastern Kentucky. He doesn't remember quite that far back, but his mother told him she used to hold him in her arms in an old Baptist church, when at the age of three he could sing in harmony with the congregation.

My daddy bought me a mandolin when I was five. He showed me three chords and said if I learned to play the thing, he'd get me a good one. Daddy had to go up to New York and when he got back three or four weeks later, I was changing chords and singing along right with it. It tickled him to death, so he went out and bought me a Martin mandolin.

Barbra Bentley

Ricky Skaggs (*front*) with Hobert Skaggs, Dorothy Skaggs, Walter Adams, and Elmer Burchett (*left to right*) in 1959

The Skaggs family moved to Goodlettsville, Tennessee, when Ricky was six. His father was working for the Tennessee Valley Authority in Paradise, Kentucky, and encouraging his son to continue with his music.

He tried to get me on *Grand Ole Opry*, but they said I was too young. A disc jockey friend really thought there was a future for me, and he got me introduced to Lester Flatt and Earl Scruggs. I was on a television show of theirs when I was seven. It was a pretty big thing for me, I guess. At least it made it big back home, anyway.

I knew I wanted to be a professional, although I didn't know I was going to be. At the time I wanted to in one way and in another way it was boring to me. Daddy wouldn't let me get out and play football or baseball because he knew what it might do to my hands and fingers—he knew how valuable they were to me. I guess if it hadn't been for him, I probably would have laid it out a long time ago, but after he kept persuading me, I saw there was a future in it.

At one point, when Skaggs was in his early teens, he and his father were playing at a square dance. There he heard a boy about his age named Keith Whitley:

I heard him and he heard me. I was singing tenor and he was singing lead. We got to talking that night and it seemed that he liked everything I liked. He came to my house a couple of weeks later and
we started singing together. It seemed as though we had been singing together for years. We both liked the Stanley Brothers' old style
of music, songs like "White Dove," "Lonesome River," and "The
Fields Have Turned Brown." Keith and I grew up the same way the
Stanleys did, in fundamentalist Baptist churches and in rough country.

One evening Whitley and Skaggs went to West Virginia to
hear Ralph Stanley. The band was late, and the producer
asked the boys to fill in:

So after we started playing, Ralph walked in. There he was standing
there listening to me instead of the other way 'round. He'd listen a
while, then drop his head. I didn't know whether he liked it or not.
But he must have liked it because he came back as soon as the band
got off stage and wanted us back on stage. He told us that our singing really brought back a lot of memories, just to hear people sing
old songs.

Ralph Stanley invited the boys back to perform the next
time he was in the area. The result was an invitation to tour
with his band during the summer.

Bluegrass-festival audiences heard Whitley and Skaggs and
found in them a reincarnation of Ralph and the late Carter
Stanley. Records followed, including an album of gospel
songs:

We all grew up in the same atmosphere and we knew a lot of those
songs. Going down the road at three o'clock in the morning, driving
the car and singing—you've got to stay awake—we'd sing those old
Baptist hymns. They came out as natural as can be for us.

Skaggs married one of Ralph's cousins, moved to Manassas,
Virginia, and started working for an electric company. But
music stayed with him. People kept asking him why he was
playing only on weekends, a question that made him reassess
his career:

Ron Petronko

Ricky Skaggs (*left*) with Keith Whitley in 1971

One night the Country Gentlemen and the Osborne Brothers were doing a show. So I went down to see it and the first guy I ran into was Bill Emerson, a very dear friend. We talked a while and he got my phone number. We started picking a little and one day he called and asked me whether I was free to do anything. He asked whether I could cut an album with the Country Gentlemen. At first I thought he was kidding. I asked, "What'll I be playing, mandolin, guitar, or something?" He said, "No, we want you to play fiddle." I couldn't believe it—the Gents never had a fiddle. But we tried it and it fit in perfectly. They really loved it.

Skaggs became a temporary member of the band while Emerson recuperated from an accident. Early in 1973 the Country Gentlemen did a concert in New York City. It was an event that altered Skaggs's career:

I'm not bragging on it, but it was a really good show. It changed my mind about things. I knew that the band was something that appealed to me more than anything else I could do. I found that I could make a living in music. The Country Gentlemen pay weekly salaries—they're a corporation and have other benefits too.

So Skaggs went back to Bluegrass on a full-time basis. From the old-time sound of the Clinch Mountain Boys to the progressive style of the Country Gentlemen, he has run the full spectrum of Bluegrass.

ROGER SPRUNG

Washington Square Park stands at the foot of New York City's Fifth Avenue, its marble arch a gateway to Greenwich Village. During the 1950s and 1960s the Park was the Grand Old Opry of New York's folk music set, and Sunday afternoons were a citybilly's dream. Musicians clustered on benches, around the wading pool, and under the arch. A teenage banjo picker, his Scruggs rolls hot out of the oven, would find willing accompanists, some of whom might be the best of the urban folk crowd.

This was the milieu of Roger Sprung. Born in 1930 in New York City, his musical experience was confined to the piano until he was sixteen years old. Then his brother took him down to the Square, where he heard someone playing a five-string banjo. It was love at first hearing.

Billy Faier, a friend of mine who had a considerable reputation as a picker, taught me the basics of Bluegrass banjo. He also showed me how to slow down records in order to hear all the notes. In those days we would play 78s at 45 RPM. The first song I worked out was "She's My Little Georgia Rose" by Flatt and Scruggs.

Some friends in Philadelphia took me to a place called the New River Ranch where Flatt and Scruggs and Don Reno were appearing. I couldn't wait to hear the music. The car was still going when I hopped out—I almost broke my neck in my eagerness.

Nineteen fifty was an important year for Sprung. He appeared on his first record, an album that included folk heroes Woody Guthrie, Cisco Huston, and Huddie "Leadbelly" Ledbetter. Also on the record were Eric Darling, later a member of the Weavers, and Bob Carey, who subsequently joined the Tarriers. Darling, Carey, and Sprung were Washington Square Park regulars, along with Eric Weissberg, Marshall Brickman, Oscar Brand, John Cohen, and many others. Their music wasn't exclusively Bluegrass, but the emphasis was on authentic rural music.

Sprung made his first southern trip in 1950, taken by mandolin player Harry West to Asheville, North Carolina. He discovered a trove of local musicians: Obray Ramsey, Byard Ray, Bascom Lamar Lunsford, Gaither Carlton, and Samantha Bumgartner. Sprung listened to these traditional pickers and singers, exploring the culture that produced and perpetuated mountain music. He then decided to make music his profession as well as his avocation.

Other trips took Sprung even deeper into Bluegrass country. He was not bashful about joining other pickers. Sprung remembers being backstage at Knoxville's WNOX: "I went up to someone and asked whether he played anything. 'Oh, I play the guitar a little,' he told me. It was Carl Story [the leader of the Rambling Mountaineers, and a noted gospel singer], and I joined him on the air. I had no idea who he was."

Making a living from folk music involved a variety of efforts. Sprung traveled to festivals and conventions, dealing in instruments and accessories. Back in New York he gave music lessons and performed at night clubs in Greenwich Village. He accompanied Jean Ritchie, whose family in Viper, Kentucky, was well known in folk circles for their renditions of ballads and play-party songs. Sprung joined Lionel Kilberg and Mike Cohen as the Shanty Boys, one of the earliest folk trios. In his travels through North Carolina, Sprung

Roger Sprung (*center*) **at Washington Square Park,
New York City, in 1950**

met the blind guitarist Doc Watson, who later was a part of
the string band on Sprung's first "Progressive Bluegrass"
album. The selections ran the gamut of country music and
beyond, from "Whistling Rufus" and "Greensleeves" to
"Mack the Knife" and "Malagueña." Sprung's interest in all
kinds of music was reflected on subsequent albums: "If I
liked a song and could fit it into a Bluegrass framework, then
I'd play it." In addition to traditional material, the band recorded arrangements of "Puff, the Magic Dragon," "Hello,
Dolly," and the Christmas song "The Little Drummer Boy."

The folk-music craze helped Sprung take Bluegrass into
unlikely places. Substituting for a colleague, he appeared in
1965 on the same bill as pop singer Kay Starr at the Persian
Room of New York City's Plaza Hotel. "One evening a fellow

requested me to play 'Smoke on the Hillside.' I had to explain that I didn't know the tune. Later on it dawned on me—he meant 'Fire on the Mountain,' which every banjo picker knows."

Another job was making a record with Guy Lombardo and his Royal Canadians, during which session Sprung remembers having to change keys in mid-song: "I had to slide the capo along the banjo's neck sometimes two or three times during a tune, and without missing a beat. It had me going some."

Sprung continued his expeditions to Asheville and other festivals. He won the 1970 Union Grove, North Carolina, Fiddlers' Convention title of "World's Champion Banjo Player." "The contest began at three in the afternoon, and I was one of the first to play. I guess the judges remembered me pretty well, because the competition went on until after ten o'clock."

Washington Square has proved to be a fertile training group for urban pickers. Eric Weissberg and Marshall Brickman went on to be members of the Tarriers, and Weissberg's banjo playing was heard as the "Dueling Banjos" segment of *Deliverance*. Other "Square" alumni remained in Bluegrass, but few have shown the tenacity of Roger Sprung. He continues to buy and sell instruments, give lessons, record, and perform. Last winter Bill Monroe and the Blue Grass Boys shared a concert with Roger Sprung and the Progressive Bluegrassers. Fittingly enough, the show took place in an auditorium almost in the shadow of the Washington Square arch.

EIGHT ᴘARKING LOT PICKERS
AND OTHER FOLKS

Finding Bluegrass is, in most parts of the media pasture, a difficult chore. Even the most obvious places turn out to be slim pickings. Take radio, for example. Although Bluegrass is a part of rural music, the "top forty" country stations play it infrequently when they play it at all. Program directors offer several explanations. First of all, the country-music industry is so busy promoting a cosmopolitan "modern image" that, even though many progressive and "rock-Bluegrass" groups are indistinguishable from the Nashville Sound, banjos and fiddles are still viewed as "hayseed," and most Bluegrass records sent to stations are summarily plowed under. Presented with the argument that string-band music amounts to at least five per cent of total country record sales, programmers fall back on an old and hollow argument. They don't want to take the risk of playing it even once every few hours. "People might switch stations," they say, "and then where would we—and our sponsors—be?"

There are several 50,000-watt stations in the South that are exceptions to the rule, especially those that have figured prominently in the history of string-band music. Jamborees, barn dances, and the venerable *Grand Ole Opry* continue to play Bluegrass without jeopardizing commercial sponsorship. Reluctant program managers might take a cue, for example, from *Grand Ole Opry*, which continues to include Bill Monroe and the Blue Grass Boys, Jim and Jesse, and the Earl Scruggs Revue. Audiences beyond the range of such stations also have their sources, thanks to the interest of young people. Listener-sponsored and college FM stations have old-time and Bluegrass shows. They are informal affairs where disc jockeys encourage requests from listeners, provide news of nearby concerts, and sometimes present live performances and tapes of local bands.

Locating records is somewhat easier. Until a few years ago any shops that bothered to stock Bluegrass lumped them under "Country Music" or "Folk" headings (one store's manager placed a banjo album in the "International" category when he saw the "funny-looking guitar" on the jacket). Now, because of the music's increased popularity, many stores feature separate "Bluegrass" racks, often with individual bins for Bill Monroe, Lester Flatt, Earl Scruggs, and other artists. But it all seems to depend on the interest of the owners and the demands of their clientele, with occasional promotional shoves from record companies.

The backbone of string-band music is the smaller record labels, which reissue and anthologize older records (the only way one can hear Charlie Poole, the Lonesome Pine Fiddlers, or the early Stanley Brothers), in addition to presenting the latest efforts of contemporary musicians. All of them exist primarily through mail-order sales, either directly to the purchaser or through intermediary distributors. (See the Appendix for a representative listing of available records.)

Nothing, however, matches the string-band music that is heard in concert or other forms of live performance. Night clubs and bars around the nation headline Bluegrass on a regular or occasional basis, while some regional clubs and societies sponsor Bluegrass events. Every area has a string-band grapevine, and one place to find out about what's taking place is at a string-instrument shop or folklore center (check the phone book's classified section under "Musical Instruments"). On walls laden with banjos, guitars, and other instruments for sale, you'll find posters listing string-band activities. Just ask if you don't see what you're looking for—the shop's owner or that customer hunched over a guitar in the corner will know about radio shows, record stores, and any local appearances.

Three national periodicals provide a more comprehensive source. *Bluegrass Unlimited, Muleskinner News,* and *Pickin'* are monthly magazines that contain interviews with musicians, record reviews, gossipy columns, and announcements of festivals and personal appearances. It's the rare Bluegrass buff who doesn't subscribe to one or more of these magazines and profit from their contents.

The Fifteen Strings Band, Bluegrass Special, and Bluegrass 45 are not particularly unusual names for groups, but their personnel include such names as Christian d'Amato and Claude Lefebvre, Wolfgang Entmyer and Willy Neefger, and Tsuyshi Otsuka and Bobby Kurakawa. The answer, quite simply, is that Bluegrass flourishes in other countries (these three groups are based, respectively, in France, Austria, and Japan). There are banjos in Budapest, mandolins in Manchester, and Scruggs-pickers in Sydney. Like other aspects of American culture, country music is popular in Europe and Asia, especially in places where our armed forces have been stationed. The Japanese are particularly keen. Festivals take place during summer months, records made by American artists are readily available, and there are more than 150 bands. Bluegrass 45 is one such group; its name refers to the year 1945 when the Blue Grass Boys consisted of its landmark personnel, including Monroe, Flatt, Scruggs, and Wise. The repertoire of Bluegrass 45 is as eclectic as that of any progressive band, including songs made famous by Joan Baez, the Bee Gees, and the Everly Brothers. But Bluegrass 45 goes beyond mere imitation. It works Oriental tonalities into these songs, as well as adapting traditional Japanese melodies into such compositions as "Fuji Mountain Backstep" and "Cherry Blossom Special." Highlight of the band's career was to come to the United States and perform at many Bluegrass fes-

Roger Sprung

Two Japanese pickers

tivals where, rather than being treated as an oddity, they were warmly accepted into the family.

American bands have toured abroad: Flatt and Scruggs, the Blue Grass Boys, and the Country Gentlemen have been well received in Europe and Asia. Especially popular in Japan, Ralph Stanley and the Clinch Mountain Boys made a trip there in 1971 and appeared at six concerts in the cities of Kyoto, Fukuoka, Osaka, and Tokyo, as well as over national radio and television programs. Audiences clamored for requests and autographs, behaving no differently from people at any American festival or concern. The Clinch Mountain Boys were joined on a radio broadcast by Japan's professional group the Tainaka Brothers. "Mountain Dew" and "Katy Cline" were as much appreciated by the audience as by the visiting Americans who learned firsthand how Bluegrass has become an international form.

There is a small but eager coterie of Bluegrass buffs in the British Isles, thanks in no small part to Bill Clifton. Clifton moved to England in 1963 after having been active in American Bluegrass circles for many years. He performs occasionally with a band composed of visiting firemen from the States and pickers summoned from other parts of Britain and the Continent. Clifton was instrumental in having Bill Monroe and the Blue Grass Boys appear at an annual country-and-western music festival at the Wembley Pool stadium in London, and through Clifton's good offices, the band's fiddler Kenny Baker is looking forward, after the 1975 engagement, to trading licks with several traditional fiddlers of Scotland's Western Isles.

When the Woodstock rock-music festival took place, much was made of the thousands of people who endured rough weather and even rougher conditions to be a part of their favorite kind of music. Bluegrass fans were not surprised. They were already used to outdoor gatherings, which may be less populous and flamboyant than Woodstock, but are no less intense in terms of audience appreciation.

String-band gatherings first took place on an informal basis as neighbors got together for picking and singing. The occasion was often a corn husking or barn raising where music made the work go faster and the respite more enjoyable. Fiddlers' conventions arose after the Civil War and became annual events for competitors from the same area. In 1965, however, Bluegrass finally found a contemporary and enduring outlet. A promoter named Carlton Haney staged a three-day event in Fincastle, Virginia, to honor Bill Monroe and past and present Blue Grass Boys. The idea of weekend en-

campments devoted to pickin' and singin' caught on and over
the years, almost in geometric progression, festivals prolifer-
ated. At last count there are now 70 Bluegrass festivals
and 110 fiddlers' conventions and folk festivals in the United
States. Held from April through November, they take place
from Maine to California and from Washington State to
Florida. Some include amateur talent competitions, instrument instruction workshops, and crafts exhibitions. Some
are confined to old-time music, while others feature progressive bands. Urban settings are not unknown: one takes place
in the shadow of New York's Wall Street skyscrapers, and
another beside the Smithsonian Institution in Washington,
D.C. Most, however, take place in rural areas, with Virginia
and North Carolina appropriately well represented. Major
performers lend their names and presence to certain events:
Bill Monroe in Bean Blossom, Indiana; Lester Flatt in Mt.
Pilot, North Carolina; and Ralph Stanley in Coeburn, Virginia, for example. But regardless of the setting or the partici-
pants, each is an opportunity for the Bluegrass clan to gather.

A festival typically takes place over an entire weekend on
grounds encompassing many acres of land suitable for camp-
ing. The audience begins to arrive on Friday afternoon,
quickly lining the road with their cars, trucks, and campers.
No sooner do people reach the ground than they unpack their
instruments, raring to locate others with whom to make
music. This aspect goes to the very heart of festivals, and
indeed of Bluegrass itself. "Parking lot picker" is the term for
an amateur who not only listens to Bluegrass, but who plays
it. They're the people who willingly travel hundreds of miles
to attend concerts and festivals and who follow the music as
closely as stockbrokers scrutinize tickertape. Their comments
can be devastatingly critical in their honesty and they make
no bones about telling professional musicians what they
think. "Hey, John," said one to a sideman, "wanna give me
back the five bucks I paid for that new album? You were lay-

Steve Arkin

Scenes of a Bluegrass festival

ing back on every cut—man, I heard the same licks from you ten years ago!"

When the bands' buses pull up, it's as though the circus has come to town. Fans cluster around favorites, expressing their admiration and requesting tunes, while the professionals greet friends and sign autographs. As the dinner hour approaches, the aroma of charcoal lazily spreads across the campgrounds, and then the crowd gathers at a wooden-plank bandstand for the evening concert. Whines of overtired children and tape recorders mix with the sound of folding chairs being set up. If the festival is under the aegis of a "name" musician, he welcomes the audience and introduces the acts, whose songs release rebel yells of pent-up enthusiasm. Each band does a set of fifteen or twenty minutes. "Here's a tune we do on our latest album," is a bandleader's typical introduction. "We'll be selling copies throughout the weekend, so don't forget to buy a fistful." The show ends, and spectators wend their way back to tents, trailers, and sleeping bags.

"Charlie! You never get up this early at home," a woman chides her husband the next morning. After several years of festival-going, she should have become accustomed to her weekend status as a Bluegrass-roots widow. Wolfing down his coffee, Charlie wastes no time in grabbing his banjo and leaving the family's trailer in search of other pickers. He pauses to hear a group already in action near the bandstand. It sounds far too expert for him, so he gravitates toward another over the hill alongside a stream. Without losing a beat, they step back to let him in. At the end of the tune, Charlie asks another banjo picker to show him a lick which had caught his ear, and the two men withdraw for a quick instruction period. Then, as the session continues, others drift up, including the sidemen of a name band. Professionals have no reluctance about "sitting in" with parking lot pickers, without feeling a need to show off or outshine their colleagues of the moment. Amateurs find the company stimulating and find

Clark Thomas

Buck Graves shows a young picker a few licks

that they are spurred on to play in ways they never knew they could. This kind of spontaneity and camaraderie marks any festival. Pickers pick and trade licks, listeners listen, vendors sell their wares, and friends gossip, all in a relaxed atmosphere and admixture of lifestyles. Long hair or crew cuts, bare feet or polished shoes, wash-and-wear shirts or tie-dyed tank tops, urban accents or rural drawls—the highest common denominator is a passion for Bluegrass.

Lunchtime may be followed by a series of workshops where professionals and talented amateurs lead seminars in the intricacies of their instruments. If there is a competition, banjo pickers, fiddlers, and string bands line up in the wings, nervous as Golden Gloves contenders. Instruments, cash awards, and perhaps the chance to perform at the evening's concert are the prizes. Contestants range in age from youngsters, knee-high to a bass fiddle, to eighty-year old-timers.

The highlight of every festival weekend is the Saturday night performance. The procession of performers can range from the most traditionally based band to a group of electric-rock "New-Grass" boys. A frequent finale to the concert is groups of well-known musicians reunited to do songs they made famous when, perhaps a decade ago, they belonged to the same organization.

No Sunday morning, especially in the South, is complete without a religious service. The congregation is led by a local minister and gospel-oriented bands provide sacred songs. No one is in any particular hurry to leave the festival grounds. The last pickers reluctantly pack their banjos and guitars to face another week or perhaps a month of solo playing, listening to tapes and records, and the memories of the weekend.

Most festivals involve roughing it, a decided strain on anyone whose notions of the good life may be found in advertisements for Hilton Hotels. But Port-O-Sans and muddy cow pastures mean little to dyed-in-the-wool Bluegrass fans, many of whom plan their year around dozens of festivals, some more than a day's drive from home. After all, string-band music came from migration, adaptation, and improvisation, and a festival offers a mini-history of the music's antecedents. Bluegrass knows where it's been, where it is, and if the future seems at times somewhat speculative, no one seems to worry. Whether on stage or clustered in parking lots, its practitioners are too busy making music.

APPENDIX

The albums referred to in this section are the most important or the most representative of the types of music discussed in the chapters in this book. I haven't tried to include everything, only because many of the records are simply not available and I wanted to avoid sending readers out on wild-goose chases for too many out-of-print or hard-to-locate records. Also included in these notes are listings of clubs, magazines, relevant books, and sources for some of the material I have incorporated into this book.

ONE: THEY CALL IT BLUEGRASS
As an introduction to the subject, I offer the following records as representative of the evolution and present state of string-band music:

Early Rural String Bands (RCA 552), a reissue of the first country-music recordings up to the Monroe Brothers, and *Early Blue Grass* (RCA LPV 569), which continues through the 1950s, together provide a mini-history of string-band music.

The High Lonesome Sound of Bill Monroe (Decca 74780) captures the vocal and instrumental virtuosity of the Blue Grass Boys during the formative years of Bluegrass.

Country Music (Mercury 20358) is the premier Flatt and Scruggs album and the novice banjo-pickers' primer. Hard to locate, it's well worth the search.

Mountain Music Bluegrass Style (Folkways 2318) is an anthology of professional and semi-pro pickers. Their ability and enthusiasm come through in a thoroughly engaging fashion.

The Country Gentlemen (Vanguard VSD 79331) is "progressive Bluegrass" as performed by its best-known exponents. You'll hear how string bands can make good use of songs from country and allied categories.

Along similar lines, *Will the Circle Be Unbroken* (United Artists UAS 9801) blends the Nitty Gritty Dirt Band, a country-rock group, with several well-known country musicians. In addition to Roy Acuff, Merle Travis, and Mother Maybelle Carter, the three-record set includes Earl Scruggs, Jimmy Martin, and Doc Watson in good-time back-porch pickin' and singin'.

Bean Blossom (MCA 2-8002) was recorded during one of Bill Monroe's Bluegrass festivals and features most of the major bands in live performances.

TWO: UP IN THE HILLS

The Library of Congress has issued several albums which contain field recordings of traditional balladry, among which are *Anglo-American Ballads* (Library of Congress Records 1) and *Anglo-American Songs and Ballads* (LC 2). See also *Jean Ritchie British Ballads* (Folkways 2301 and 2302). Unaccompanied ballads are found on *Ballads and Breakdowns from the Southern Mountains* (Prestige International 25003) and *Old Time Music at Clarence Ashley's* (Folkways FA 2355, and Vol. 2 FA 2358). Richard Dyer-Bennett and John Jacob Niles have recorded ballads in artful arrangements.

There's no dearth of old-time fiddle music. Try *American Fiddle Tunes* (Library of Congress 62), "The Scotch Musick" on *Ballads and Breakdowns from the Southern Mountains* (Prestige International 25003), and "Leather Britches" and "Natchez Under the Hill" (both with banjo accompaniment) on *Mountain Music Bluegrass Style* (Folkways FA 2318).

The Reindeau Family (County 725) has a number of Scots-Irish reels. Contemporary Irish and Scottish popular music includes reels, hornpipes, and jigs—check the "International" bins at record shops. Then too, few Bluegrass albums omit at least one cut based on centuries-old tunes.

"Amazing Grace" on *Old Time Music at Clarence Ashley's* (Folkways 2358) shows the influence of shaped-note singing. An entire album, *Sacred Harp Singing* (Library of Congress 11) is devoted to that form. Parallel harmonies and "after-beat" syncopation are most pronounced in gospel numbers as performed by the Blue Grass Boys, the Stanley Brothers, the Tennessee Cut-Ups, and the Lewis Family.

Play-party songs are included on *Songs and Games of the Southern Mountains* by Jean Ritchie (Folkways 7054) and the New Lost City Ramblers' *Old Timey Songs for Children* (Folkways 7064).

Among the many albums containing examples of two-finger and clawhammer banjo picking are *Mountain Banjo Songs and Tunes* (County 215) and *Folk Banjo Styles* (Elektra EKL-217). *Clawhammer Banjo* (County 701) focuses on the latter style, and to see it being performed, look for Grandpa Jones on the television show *Hee Haw*.

For examples of other instruments, see *Old Time Mountain Guitar* (County 523) and *Mountain Music Played on the Autoharp* (Folkways FA 2365).

A scholarly examination of modal forms and other facets of mountain music may be found in *Anglo-American Folksong Styles* by Roger D. Abrahams and George Foss (Prentice-Hall, 1968). Another useful book is *The Viking Book of Folk Ballads of the English-Speaking World,* edited by Albert B. Friedman (Viking, 1956).

THREE: RIGHT INTO THE MICROPHONE

Much of the music made during or based on this formative commercial era is available. A three-volume set on Folkways, *Anthology of American Folk Music* (FA 2951, 2952, and 2953), is highly recommended: string bands, jug bands, and ballad and blues singers in a panorama of 1920s and 1930s music. In addition to the *Early Rural String Bands* (RCA LPV 552) mentioned previously, other collections include *Mountain Songs* (County 504) and *The String Bands, Vols. 1 and 2* (Old Timey 100 and 101).

With regard to specific performers, Eck Robertson may be found on *Old Time Fiddle Classics, Vol. 2* (County 527). Entire albums of string bands include *Gid Tanner's Skillet Lickers* (County 506), *The McGhee Brothers and Arthur Smith* (Folkways 2379), *Charlie Poole and the North Carolina Ramblers* (County 505, 506 and 516), and *J. E. Mainer's Mountaineers* (Old Timey 106 and 107 and Arhoolie 5002). The Blue Sky Boys are on *Sunny Side of Life* (Rounder 1006). Others include *Dock Boggs* (Folkways 2351), *Wade Mainer* (Old Homestead 90001 and 90002), and *Snuffy Jenkins* (Arhoolie 5011). The Morris Brothers appear on *Earl Scruggs: His Family and Friends* (Columbia C-30584) and *Old Time Music and Bluegrass At Newport* (Vanguard VRS 9146).

Examples of Negro-based music may be heard on the Folkways *Anthology* cited above, *Elizabeth Cotton* (Folkways FA 2536), and *Sounds of the South* (Atlantic 1346). Scott Joplin's ragtime piano compositions were used in the score of the motion picture *The Sting*, and for barrelhouse piano rags and blues see *Songs of Memphis Slim and Willie Dixon* (Folkways FA 2385).

Western swing is most closely identified with Bob Wills, whose *Hall of Fame* (United Artists 9962) contains his excellent fiddling.

Urban interest in the preservation and perpetuation of old-time music is in no small way attributable to the efforts of the New Lost City Ramblers. Mike Seeger, John Cohen, and Tom Paley (later replaced by Tracy Schwartz) have recreated twenties and thirties rural music with a note-for-note fidelity. The Ramblers' Folkways albums include printed notes of considerable interest and scholarship. *The New Lost City Ramblers Songbook* (Oak Publications, 1964) contains the words and music to many of the 1920s and 1930s string-band repertoire of the group.

For more on the commercial era, see *Country Music, U.S.A.* by Bill Malone (University of Texas Press, 1968). The book is a well-researched history of all forms of country-and-western music, including a chapter on Bluegrass and the urban folk revival.

FOUR: BILL MONROE AND THE BLUE GRASS BOYS

Three of Monroe's albums are particularly recommended. *Bill Monroe's Greatest Hits* (Decca DL 75010) is an anthology of songs most closely associated with him, including "Uncle Pen" and "Molly and Tenbrooks." *Bill Monroe's Uncle Pen* (Decca DL 75348) contains string-band arrangements of fiddle tunes drawn from his uncle's repertoire. *Bean Blossom* (MCA 2-8002) was recorded live at Monroe's Seventh Annual Bluegrass Festival. It shows his role as *pater-familias* and includes Jim, Jesse, and James Monroe performing with him, along with an "honor roll" of Bluegrass fiddlers in action.

Three "budget" labels have reissued albums with Monroe's early recordings. *Bluegrass Music by the Monroe Brothers* (Camden CAL 719) has Bill and Charlie's duets. *The Great Bill Monroe* (Harmony HL 2790) and *The Original Bluegrass Sound* (Harmony HL 7338) includes the Blue Grass Boys' landmark personnel: Lester Flatt, Earl Scruggs, Chubby Wise, and Mac Wiseman, although liner notes do not identify the musicians.

I Saw the Light (Decca DL 78769) and *A Voice from on High* (DL 75135) are exclusively gospel. *The High Lonesome Sound* (Decca 74780) contains vocals by Jimmy Martin and

Carter Stanley. *Bluegrass Instrumentals* (Decca DL 74601) has many of Monroe's original compositions as well as Bill Keith's chromatic-style banjo on "Sailor's Hornpipe." James Monroe joins his dad on *Father and Son* (MCA 310).

Many of the Blue Grass Boys who went on to form their own bands or join others will be mentioned in subsequent entries. Kenny Barker, long a member of Monroe's band, appears on *Portrait of a Bluegrass Fiddler* (County 719), *Baker's Dozen* (County 730), and *Kenny Baker Country* (County 736).

Three of the younger alumni set—Richard Greene, Pete Rowan, and Bill Keith—had a reunion of sorts on *Muleskinner* (Warner Brothers BS 2787). Joined by David Grisman and the late Clarence White, they play many of the Monroe standards as well as some country-rock tunes.

Interviews with Monroe and his associates form the basis of half of *Bossman: Bill Monroe and Muddy Waters*, by James Rooney (The Dial Press, 1971).

FIVE: LESTER FLATT AND EARL SCRUGGS AND THE FOGGY MOUNTAIN BOYS

The evolution of three-finger picking, from Snuffy Jenkins through Scruggs, is traced on *American Banjo Scruggs Style* (Folkways FA 2314).

The best-selling instruction book is, not surprisingly, *Earl Scruggs and the Five-String Banjo* (Peer International, 1968). Pete Seeger's *How to Play the Five-String Banjo* (published by the author, 1962) contains a chapter on the subject.

Flatt and Scruggs were among the Blue Grass Boys' personnel on *The Original Bluegrass Sound* (Harmony HL 7338) and *The Great Bill Monroe* (Harmony HL 2790).

Country Music (Mercury MG 20358) is the Foggy Mountain Boys' ur-text, full of standards like "Foggy Mountain Breakdown," "Salty Dog," "Down the Road," and "Roll in

My Sweet Baby's Arms." As the notes for Chapter One indicated, copies are hard to find, but most of the tunes have been reissued on other albums (for example, *The World of Flatt and Scruggs*, Columbia KL 31964). Two other notable albums are *Foggy Mountain Jamboree* (Columbia CL 1019) and *Foggy Mountain Banjo* (Columbia CS 8364).

The band's "middle period" was captured on *Folk Songs of Our Land* (Columbia CS 8630) and *Hard Travelin'* (Columbia CS 8751). The latter contains the *Beverly Hillbillies'* theme "The Ballad of Jed Clampett." Flatt and Scruggs were joined by Doc Watson on *Strictly Instrumental* (Columbia CS 9443) and by Mother Maybelle Carter on *Songs of the Famous Carter Family* (Columbia CS 8464). Live performances before urban and college audiences are on *Flatt and Scruggs at Carnegie Hall* (Columbia CS 8845) and *Flatt and Scruggs Recorded Live at Vanderbilt University* (Columbia CS 8934).

Among the last albums recorded by the Foggy Mountain Boys were *A Boy Named Sue* (Columbia CS 32244) and *One Last Time* (Columbia CS 9945) with songs popularized by Johnny Cash and Bob Dylan.

After Flatt and Scruggs dissolved their association, Flatt and his Nashville Grass recorded *Kentucky Ridgerunner* (RCA LSP-4633), *Foggy Mountain Breakdown* (RCA LSP-4789), and with Mac Wiseman, *Lester 'n' Mac* (RCA LSP-4547).

Scruggs' subsequent albums include *Earl Scruggs: His Family and Friends* (Columbia C-30584) based on a television documentary and with Joan Baez, Bob Dylan, the Morris Brothers, and a Moog synthesizer. He's joined by Linda Ronstadt, Arlo Guthrie, and others on *I Saw the Light* (Columbia KC 31354). The first Scruggs Revue album was *The Earl Scruggs Revue* (Columbia KC 32426). Scruggs and Vassar Clements appear on *Will the Circle Be Unbroken* (United Artists UAS 9801).

Ruby Red by William Price Fox (Lippincott, 1971) is a novel about a woman's trying to succeed as a country-music singer. Mr. Fox's appreciation of Bluegrass is evident, for his description of a Foggy Mountain Boys appearance on *Grand Ole Opry* approaches lyric poetry.

SIX: THE SPREAD OF BLUEGRASS

Since Stanley Brothers' albums are found on smaller labels, locating them requires something of an effort (although well worth the trouble). If you draw a blank at your local record shop, order through Rounder Records or County Sales, whose addresses are given in the notes to Chapter Eight. For openers, there's *The Stanley Brothers: Their Early Recordings* (Melodeon MLP 7322). *The Stanley Brothers of Virginia, Vols.* 1 and 2 (County 738 and 739) are fine examples of the Clinch Mountain Boys' "high lonesome" sound. *The Legendary Stanley Brothers* (Rebel SLP 1487) took place before an enthusiastic audience, and *The Stanley Brothers: Together for the Last Time* (Rebel SLP 1512) was recorded shortly before Carter's death.

Ralph Stanley and the Clinch Mountain Boys have a number of albums on Rebel, including *Something Old, Something New* (1508), *Play Requests* (1514), and a collection of sacred songs *Cry from the Cross* (1499).

The Ralph Stanley Fan Club is the most active of such organizations. For particulars, including membership in a tape club, contact Fay McGinnis, 1156 21st Street, Wyandotte, Michigan 48192.

Jimmy Martin's albums on Decca (now MCA) show the consistency which has become his hallmark. *Moonshine Hollow* (DL 20010), *Good 'n' Country* (DL 4016), *Big 'n' Country Instrumentals* (DL 47891), and *Widow Maker* (DL 74536) are all representative. Martin can also be heard on *Early Blue Grass* (RCA LPV-569) with the Osborne Brothers, and on *Will the Circle Be Unbroken* (United Artists UAS 9801).

Don Reno's albums also must be purchased through record sales services. On the King label are *The Best of Reno and Smiley* (1091), *The Fastest Five String Alive* (1065), *Tally Ho* (731051), *Instruments and Ballads* (579), and *Country Songs* (701). Two other albums on two other labels are *Reno and Harrell* (Rural Rhythm 171) and *Bluegrass Favorites* (Jalyn 108). There's some dazzling twin banjo work on *Eddie Adcock and Don Reno* (Rebel SPL 1482).

Among Jim and Jesse McReynolds' earliest albums are *Bluegrass Special* (Epic LN 24031) and *Bluegrass Classics* (Epic LN 24074). Rock 'n' roll done string-band style is on *Berry Pickin' in the Country* (Epic BN 26176), their arrangements of Chuck Berry songs. Jim and Jesse acknowledge the influence of an earlier fraternal duet on *Saluting the Louvin Brothers* (Epic BN 26465). *We Like Trains* (Epic 26513) is solid country music, complete with electric guitar and trumpet (the latter provided by Danny Davis, leader of the Nashville Brass). That Jesse can handle another instrument is demonstrated on *Me and My Fiddles* (Atteiram API-1030). The McReynolds appear in concert on *Country Music and Bluegrass at Newport* (Vanguard VSD 79146) and *Bean Blossom* (MCA 2-8002).

The Osborne Brothers appear with Jimmy Martin on *Early Blue Grass* (RCA LPV-569). Examples of their "modern" Bluegrass are found on *Ru-be-eeee* (Decca 75204), *Midnight Flyer* (MCA 311), and *Country Roads* (Decca 75321). *Blue Grass Express* (MCA Coral CB-20003) contains previously recorded selections from five other albums. *The Osborne Brothers* (Decca DL 75271) runs the gamut of country music from Hank Williams songs to "Georgia Pineywood" written by Felice and Boudeleaux Bryant. Their recent album, *Fastest Grass Alive* (MCA 374) takes them back to more traditional Bluegrass.

Among the Lewis Family's albums recorded for Starday are *The Best of the Lewis Family* (SLP 465) and *Golden Gospel*

Best of the Lewis Family (SLP 450). Their Nashville label albums are slightly easier to locate: *Singing Time Down South* (NLP 2016), *The Gospel Singing Sensations from Dixie* (NLP 2062), and *The Lewis Family Takes You to a Gospel Sing-Out* (NLP 2045). They now record on Canaan and have done among others *Lewis Country* (CAS 9690-LP), *Just Us* (CAS 9720-LP), and *The Lewis Family Lives in a Happy World* (CAS 9738-LP). Little Roy's banjo sparkles on *Golden Gospel Banjo* (Starday SLP 422) and *Gospel Banjo* (Canaan CAS 9722-LP).

If sacred music gets into your soul (or vice versa), look for *Sixteen Gospel Songs, Vols. 1, 2, and 3* (Rimrock 308, 1003, and 3004) with Flatt and Scruggs, the Stanley Brothers, Reno and Smiley, and Charlie Monroe. Bill Monroe, Carl Story, Flatt and Scruggs, the Stanley Brothers, the Country Gentlemen, Reno and Harrell, and the Rainey Family are among the many individuals and groups who include gospel songs in their repertoire.

The Country Gentlemen, Vols. 1, 2, and 3 (Folkways FA 2409, 2410, and 2411) were recorded in the early 1960s and feature the band's original personnel, along with *The Best of the Early Country Gentlemen* (Rebel SLP 1494). Three other highly regarded albums on Rebel are *The Traveler* (SLP-1481), *Bringing Mary Home* (SLP-1478), and *The Award Winning Country Gentlemen* (SLP-1506), the last of which won *Muleskinner News* album-of-the-year designation for 1972. The group's most recent album is *The Country Gentlemen* (Vanguard VSD 79331).

Among other groups regarded as "progressive" are the New Shades of Grass, the Seldom Scene, Emerson and Waldron, and the Country Gazette. Categorization (as much as it matters) becomes more difficult when rock bands lay aside their electrified instruments in favor of banjos and mandolins: the Nitty Gritty Dirt Band, the Byrds, and the New Riders of the Purple Sage, are some that do. The Dillards started in true Bluegrass and have crossed the line into country-rock, much in the manner of the Osborne Brothers.

Getting back to traditional musicians, fiddlers don't often have the chance to step into the spotlight for more than a solo break. In addition to Kenny Baker's records mentioned in the notes to Chapter Three, the following four albums give them that opportunity. Curly Ray Cline, formerly a member of the Lonesome Pine Fiddlers and now with the Clinch Mountain Boys, is featured on *Chicken Reel* (Rebel SLP-1498) and *Little Home in West Virginia* (Rebel SLP-1515). Buck Ryan, a member of the Tennessee Cutups, can be heard on *Fiddlin' Buck Ryan* (Rural Rhythm 244). Vassar Clements is on *Southern Country Waltzes* (Rural Rhythm 236) and, with Josh Graves and most of the past and present Country Gentlemen, on *Mike Auldridge Dobro* (Takoma / Devi D-1033).

This is a likely place at least to acknowledge some of the other well-known Bluegrass artists and bands that have recorded and performed over the past quarter of a century: Red Allen, Hylo Brown, Bill Clifton, J. D. Crowe, Jim Eanes, the Goins Brothers, the Lonesome Pine Fiddlers, Wilma Lee and Stoney Cooper, the Lilly Brothers, Ted Lundy, Mac MaGaha, Red Rector, Larry Sparks, Carl Story, the Stoneman Family, the Sullivan Family, Clarence "Tater" Tate, Earl Taylor, and Rual Yarborough.

SEVEN: THREE PICKERS

The material on Vic Jordan is based on an interview conducted by David Robinson and is included by his permission. The material on Ricky Skaggs is adapted from an article by the author and is included with the permission of *Pickin'* magazine.

In addition to Vic Jordan's work on albums by the bands of which he was a member (e.g., with Jim and Jesse McReynolds on *Bean Blossom*), he accompanies Kenny Baker on *Portrait of a Bluegrass Fiddler* (County 719) and Red Rector on

Ballads and Instrumentals (Old Homestead OHS 900029). Jordan is the featured performer on *Pickaway* (Atteiram API-1027). When you hear a banjo on a "Nashville Sound" country record, chances are it's Bobby Thompson, who may also be found on *Arthur Smith—Battling Banjos* (Epic Z 32259).

Ricky Skaggs is on *Whitley and Skaggs: Tribute to the Stanley Brothers* (Jalyn 129) and again with Keith Whitley on *Second Generation Bluegrass* (Rebel SLP 1504). Among his recordings with the Clinch Mountain Boys are *Cry from the Cross* (Rebel SLP 1499) and *Ralph Stanley—Old Country Church* (Rebel SLP 1508), both of which contain some of the sacred songs to which the text refers. Skaggs is also on *The Country Gentlemen* (Vanguard VSD 79331).

Roger Sprung's earliest albums were on the Folkways label: *Progressive Bluegrass, Vol. I* (FA 2370), *Progressive Ragtime Bluegrass, Vol. II* (FA 2371), *Progressive Bluegrass 5-String Specialities, Vol. III* (FA 2472), and *Grassy Licks, Vol. IV* (FV 9037). "18th Century Drawing Room" on *Grassy Licks* is an arrangement of the Mozart C Major Piano Sonata. Joan Sprung's singing is featured on *Pickin' on the Sunnyside* (Showcase S-2) and *Roger and Joan* (Showcase S-3). To order these and his other albums, as well as for information about buying or selling instruments, write to Roger Sprung, 255 West 88 Street, New York, NY 10024.

A well-known "urban picker," Eric Weissberg, plays the *Deliverance* theme on *Dueling Banjos* (Warner Brothers 2683) and is on *Folk Banjo Styles* (Elektra EKL-217) along with Marshall Brickman and Tom Paley.

One of the first groups to spread the Bluegrass gospel during the fifties' folk revival was the Greenbriar Boys. Two of their albums still in print are *Ragged but Right* (Vanguard 79159) and *Better Late Than Never* (Vanguard 79233).

Although not a Bluegrass musician (in the Monrovian sense), Doc Watson has become an important figure in string-band music. He was a member of the group featured on the *Clarence Ashley's* albums mentioned in the notes to Chapter Three. He appeared on an album with Flatt and Scruggs referred to in the notes to Chapter Five, as well as being a part of the oft-cited *Will the Circle Be Unbroken* cast of characters. His reputation is clear to all who have heard him play: Watson's flat-picking is breathtaking. Among his many excellent albums are *Good Deal* (Vanguard Van. 79276) and *On Stage* (Vanguard VSD-9/10). That the guitar has moved from a rhythm to a lead instrument in Bluegrass is directly attributable to Doc Watson.

EIGHT: PARKING LOT PICKERS AND OTHER FOLKS

The two primary mail-order services which offer stringband records are County Sales, Box 191, Floyd, VA 24091; and Rounder Records, 186 Willow, Somerville, MA 02144. Other catalogues you'll want to have on hand are from the Library of Congress, Music Division, Recording Laboratory, Washington, DC 20540; and Folkways Records, 701 Seventh Avenue, New York, NY 10036.

The three Bluegrass magazines are *Bluegrass Unlimited* ($6.00 per year, Box 111, Burke, VA 22015), *Muleskinner News* ($7.00 per year, Rt. 2, Box 304, Elon College, NC 27244), and *Pickin'* ($6.00 per year, 1 Saddle Road, Cedar Knolls, NJ 07927). Another allied periodical is *Sing Out* (33 West 60 Street, New York, NY 10019), which contains articles about Bluegrass, old-timey music, blues, and contemporary folk music.

Oak Publications (an affiliate of *Sing Out* magazine) offers a number of books of interest to parking lot pickers. Highly recommended are *Bluegrass Banjo* by Peter Wernick and *Bluegrass Fiddle* by Gene Lowinger. Instruction books on Bluegrass guitar and mandolin are scheduled for fall 1974. Those who want to learn the techniques of pre-Bluegrass fiddling should consult *Appalachian Fiddle* by Miles Krassen and *The Fiddle Book* by Marion Thede, while their banjo counterparts can cluster around *Old-Time Mountain Banjo* by Artie Rosenbaum.

The Japanese band Bluegrass 45 has been recorded on three albums by Rebel Records: *Bluegrass 45* (SLP-1502), *The Bluegrass 45* (SLP-1516), and *Caravan* (SLP-1507). Also from across the seas comes *Old Time Music*, a British magazine available from its publishers ($4.00, 33 Brunswick Gardens, London W8, 4AW England) and through County Sales or Rounder.

Bluegrass Unlimited, Muleskinner News, and *Pickin'* are useful sources for information about festivals, conventions, and folk festivals. "Bluegrass Summer," a special annual edition of *Muleskinner News,* is the most complete and handy guide to the circuit.

The sounds and sometimes the flavor of festivals comes through recordings, such as the *37th Old Time Fiddlers Convention at Union Grove* (Folkways FA 2434) and *The Galax Fiddlers Convention* (Folkways FA 2435). Yankee jamborees were captured on *Country Music and Bluegrass at Newport* (Vanguard VRS-9146) and *Old Time Music at Newport* (Vanguard VRS-9147). And, to bring the circle full 'round, an album mentioned in the notes to Chapter One and Chapter Four fits in here too. *Bean Blossom* (MCA 2-8002) was recorded at Bill Monroe's Indiana festival. It contains Monroe, Lester Flatt, Jim and Jesse McReynolds, James Monroe, and Jimmy Martin, along with fiddlers Buck Ryan, Kenny Baker, Curly Ray Cline, Tex Logan, and Paul Warren (among others). All that's lacking to give a rounded view of string band music is a cut or two of parking lot pickers in action, which maybe some day a record producer will see fit to include.